FACSIMILE, REDUCED, OF "THE SPECTATOR,"
No. 405, SATURDAY, JUNE 14, 1712.

The type page of the original is 9¼ inches high, 6¼ inches
wide; the paper itself is 12¼ inches high, 8 inches wide.

The SPECTATOR.

Οἱ ἢ παιμμέριοι μολπῇ θεὸν ἱλάσκοντό,
Καλὸν ἀείδοντες παιῆονα κῦροι Ἀχαιῶν;
Μέλποντες Ἑκάεργον. ὁ ἢ φρένα τέρπετ᾽ ἀκέων.   Hom.

Saturday, June 14. 1712.

I Am very forry to find, by the Opera Bills for this Day, that we are likely to lofe the greatelt Performer in Dramatick Mufick that is now living, or that perhaps ever appeared upon a Stage. I need not acquaint my Reader, that I am fpeaking of *Signior Nicolini.* The Town is highly obliged to that Excellent Artift, for having fhewn us the *Italian* Mufick in its Perfection, as well as for that generous Approbation he lately gave to an Opera of our own Country, in which the Compofer endeavoured to do Juftice to the Beauty of the Words, by following that Noble Example, which has been fet him by the greateft Foreign Mafters in that Art.

I could heartily wifh there was the fame Application and Endeavours to cultivate and improve our Church-Mufick, as have been lately beftowed on that of the Stage. Our Compofers have one very great Incitement to it: they are fure to meet with Excellent Words, and, at the fame time, a wonderful Variety of them. There is no Paffion that is not finely expreffed in thofe parts of the Infpired Writing, which are proper for Divine Songs and Anthems.

There is a certain Coldnefs and Indifference in the Phrafes of our *European* Languages, when they are compared with the Oriental Forms of Speech; and it happens very luckily, that the *Hebrew* Idioms run into the *Englifh* Tongue with a particular Grace and Beauty. Our Language has received innumerable Elegancies and Improvements, from that Infufion of *Hebraifms*, which are derived to it out of the Poetical Paffages in Holy Writ. They give a Force and Energy to our Expreffions, warm and animate our Language, and convey our Thoughts in more ardent and intenfe Phrafes, than any that are to be met with in our own Tongue. There is fomething fo pathetick in this kind of Diction, that it often fets the Mind in a Flame, and makes our Hearts born within us. How cold and dead does a Prayer appear, that is compofed in the moft Elegant

and Polite Forms of Speech, which are natural to our Tongue, when it is not heightened by that Solemnity of Phrafe, which may be drawn from the Sacred Writings. It has been faid by fome of the Ancients, that if the Gods were to talk with Men, they would certainly fpeak in *Plato's* Stile; but I think we may fay, with Juftice, that when Mortals converfe with their Creator, they cannot do it in fo proper a Stile as in that of the Holy Scriptures.

If any one would judge of the Beauties of Poetry that are to be met with in the Divine Writings, and examine how kindly the *Hebrew* Manners of Speech mix and incorporate with the *Englifh* Language; after having perufed the Book of Pfalms, let him read a literal Tranflation of *Horace* or *Pindar.* He will find in thefe two laft fuch an Abfurdity and Confufion of Stile with fuch a Comparative Poverty of Imagination, as will make him very fenfible of what I have been here advancing.

Since we have therefore fuch a Treafury of Words, fo beautiful in themfelves, and fo proper for the Airs of Mufick, I cannot but wonder that Perfons of Diftinction fhould give fo little Attention and Encouragement to that kind of Mufick, which would have its Foundations in Reafon, and which would improve our Virtue in proportion as it raifed our Delight. The Paffions that are excited by ordinary Compofitions, generally flow from fuch filly and abfurd Occafions, that a Man is afhamed to reflect upon them ferioufly; but the Fear, the Love, the Sorrow, the Indignation that are awakened in the Mind by Hymns and Anthems, make the Heart better, and proceed from fuch Caufes as are altogether reafonable and praife-worthy. Pleafure and Duty go hand in hand, and the greater our Satisfaction is, the greater is our Religion.

Mufick among thofe who were ftiled the chofen People was a Religious Art. The Songs of *Sion,* which we have reafon to believe were in high repute,

pute among the Courts of the Eastern Monarchs, were nothing else but Psalms and Pieces of Poetry that adored or celebrated the Supreme Being. The greatest Conqueror in this Holy Nation, after the manner of the old *Grecian* Lyricks, did not only compose the Words of his Divine Odes, but generally set them to Musick himself: After which, his Works, tho' they were consecrated to the Tabernacle, became the National Entertainment, as well as the Devotion of his People.

The first Original of the Drama was a Religious Worship consisting only of a Chorus, which was nothing else but an Hymn to a Deity. As Luxury and Voluptuousness prevailed over Innocence and Religion, this form of Worship degenerated into Tragedies; in which however the Chorus so far remembered its first Office, as to brand every thing that was vicious, and recommend every thing that was laudable, to intercede with Heaven for the Innocent, and to implore its Vengeance on the Criminal.

Homer and *Hesiod* intimate to us how this Art should be applied, when they represent the Muses as surrounding *Jupiter*, and warbling their Hymns about his Throne. I might shew, from innumerable Passages in Ancient Writers, not only that Vocal and Instrumental Musick were made use of in their Religious Worship, but that their most favourite Diversions were filled with Songs and Hymns to their respective Deities. Had we frequent Entertainments of this Nature among us, they won't not a little purifie and exalt our Passions, give our Thoughts a proper Turn, and cherish those Divine Impulses in the Soul, which every one feels that has not stifled them by sensual and immoderate Pleasures.

Musick, when thus applied, raises noble Hints in the Mind of the Hearer, and fills it with great Conceptions. It strengthens Devotion, and advances Praise into Rapture. It lengthens out every act of Worship, and produces more lasting and permanent Impressions in the Mind, than those which accompany any transient Form of Words that are uttered in the ordinary Method of Religious Worship.

ADVERTISEMENTS.

For the Benefit of the Box-Keepers.

At the Desire of several Ladies of Quality.

By Her Majesty's Company of Comedians, AT the Theatre Royal in Drury-Lane, on Tuesday next, being the 17th Day of June, will be Reviv'd, a Comedy called, The Jovial Crew: Or, the Merry Beggars, With several Entertainments of Singing and Comic-Dancing proper to the Play. To which will be added, A Farce of one Act only, call'd, The Stage-Coach, by Her Majesty's Command, no Persons are to be admitted behind the Scenes. And on Thursday next will be presented, a Play call'd the Indian Emperor, or the Conquest of Mexico by the Spaniards, for the Benefit of Mr. Bickerstaff and Mr. Newmin.

AT the Queen's Theatre in the Hay-Market, this present Saturday being the 14th Day of June, Signior Cavaliero Nicolino Grimaldi will take his leave of England, in the Opera of Antiochus, and by reason of the Hot Weather, the Waits Fall will Play all the time. Boxes 8 s. Pit 5 s. First Gallery 2 s. 6 d. Upper Gallery 1 s. 6 d. Begins upon the Stage half a Guinea. To begin exactly at seven.

This Day is Publish'd,

The third Vol. of the Iliad of Homer, with Notes by Madam Dacier, done from the French by Mr. Broome of St. John's Colledge in Cambridge, and by him compared with the Greek. Illustrated with Cuts. Note, The 4th and 5th Vol. with a compleat Table to the five Vols. are in the Press, and will be Publish'd in July next by Bernard Lintott at the Cross Keys between the two Temple Gates in Fleetstreet: Of whom may be had the fine Miscellany lately Published.

This Day is Published,

The whole Works of that excellent Practical Physician Dr. Thomas Sydenham, wherein are only the History of acute Diseases are treat of after the most accurate Method; but also the latest way of curing most Chronical Diseases. The 5th Edition, by J. Pechey of the Colledge of Physicians, price 5 s. The Works of Etmullerus abridg'd, or a compleat System of Physick, being a Description of all Diseases incident to Men, Women and Children, with the Method of Cure. To which is added a short account of the Animal Functions, with an exact Classis of Medicines, price 6 s. Printed for R. Wellington at the Dolphin and Crown in St. Paul's Church-yard.

Whereas John Prince, John Sadler, and William Jodrell, Mercers, at the black Lyon, in Kingstreet Covent Garden, have resolved to leave off the Mercers Trade, There are to give Notice, That at the said Shop are to be sold at very low Prices, all Sorts of the newest Fashion Gold and Silver Silks, and Atlasses, Flowered and plain Velvets, Silk Brocades, flowered and plain Sattins, Damasks, Watered Tabies, Farendines and Mohairs, Singreens, Serjenets, Persians, Silk Night Gowns, Thread Sattins, Poplins, Norwich Crapes, silk and other Druggets, Hair and Worsted Camblets, Hair Shags and Whalbones.

Just Publish'd, The Second Edition of Creation. A Philosophical Poem. Demonstrating the Existence and Providence of a God, In Seven Books, By Sir Richard Blackmore, Kt. M. D. and Fellow of the College of Physicians in London. Printed for S. Buckley, at the Dolphin in Little Britain; and J. Tonson, at Shakespear's Head over against Catherine street in the Strand.

Just Published,

A very neat Pocket Edition, in two Vols. 12mo. of the Works of Mr. Thomas Otway, containing Alcibiades, Don Carlos, Titus and Berenice, Friendship in Fashion, Souldier's Fortune in two Parts, Orphan, Caius Marius and Venice Preserved. With his Poems and Love Letters. To which is added some Account of the Life and Writings of the Author. Printed for J. Tonson at Shakespear's Head in the Strand; and Sold by W. Taylor at the Ship in Pater noster row.

The Retir'd Gard'ner, or, Dialogues between a Gentleman and a Gard'ner: Containing the Methods of Making, Ordering and Improving a Fruit and Kitchin-Garden, together with the Manner of Planting and Cultivating Flowers, Plants, Shrubs, and Under-Shrubs, necessary for the Adorning of Gardens. &c. In which is explain'd, the Art of Making and Disposing of Parterres, Arbours of Greens, Wood-Works, Arches, Columns, and other Pieces and Compartments usually found in the most beautiful Gardens of Country-Seats. The whole enrich'd with Variety of Figures being a Translation from the Sieur Louis Liger, To which is add a Description and Plan of Count Tallard's Garden at Nottingham. The whole Reviv'd, with several Alterations and Additions as which render it proper for our English Culture. By George London, and Henry Wise. Printed for Jacob Tonson at Shakespear's Head over against Catherine street in the Strand.

The Works of Mr. Francis Beaumont and Mr. John Fletcher, in 7 Vols. Several never I wish Cuts, Plutarch's Lives in 5 Vols. translated by several hands, Seneca's Morals translated by Sir Roger l' Estrange. The Satyrs of Decimus Junius Juvenalis &c. translated into English Verse by Mr. Dryden and several other eminent Hands. The Works of Mr. Congreve in 3 Vols. consisting of his Plays and Poems, Prince of several Occasions written by Mr. Prior. Paradise lost, a Poem, in 12 Books, by Mr. John Milton. The Christian Hero, written by Mr. Steele, N.B. The three last are printed with a new Elzivir Letter in small Pocket Volumes: All Printed for Jacob Tonson at Shakespear's head over against Catherine street in the Strand.

Letters and Negotiations of the Count D' Estrades Ambassador from Lewis the Fourteenth to the States General of the United Provinces of the Low Countries: From the Year 1663 to the Year 1669, Consisting chiefly of Original Letters and Instructions from the French King, and his Ministers, to the said Count; with his Answers. Wherein are several secret Transactions between the Courts of England and France during that time. Translated by several Hands. In Three Volumes. Printed for D. Brown, J. Tonson, A. and J. Churchill, J. Knapton, R. Knaplock, G. Strahan, B. Bunger, and J. Pemberton.

LONDON: Printed for *Sam. Buckley*, at the *Dolphin* in *Little-Britain*; and Sold by *A. Baldwin* in *Warwick-Lane*; where Advertisements are taken in: as also by *Charles Lillie*, Perfumer, at the Corner of *Beauford-Buildings* in the Strand

O

The Riverside Literature Series

THE

SIR ROGER DE COVERLEY
PAPERS

*SELECTED FROM THE SPECTATOR AND EDITED
WITH AN INTRODUCTION AND NOTES*

HOUGHTON, MIFFLIN AND COMPANY
Boston: 4 Park Street; New York: 11 East Seventeenth Street
Chicago: 378-388 Wabash Avenue
The Riverside Press, Cambridge

CONTENTS.

INTRODUCTION.

THE frontispiece to this volume [1] gives on a reduced scale the general appearance of a folio sheet which appeared in London on the first day of March, 1710–1711,[2] was issued daily until December 6, 1712, when it was discontinued for a year and a half, resumed June 18, 1714, and then issued three times a week until December 20 of the same year, when it ceased altogether. A daily paper, it resembled the modern daily paper only in having advertisements on the same sheet, but these were few and unobtrusive. It was in effect far more comparable with the modern magazine, for it left news and politics and trade to the general newspaper, which was then beginning to assert itself, and occupied itself with criticism on books, comments on fashions and manners, and, what interests us most, attempts at character drawing and portraits of typical personages.

The "Spectator" is chief among the papers of its class which occupied the central position in literature in the eighteenth century, and it holds its high place

[1] Published through the courtesy of the Lenox Library, New York, where the original is preserved.

[2] In the former half of the eighteenth century it was still common to treat the 25th of March as New Year's Day. In order, therefore, to indicate the precise year of the days between January 1 and March 25, it was customary to write the double year date as 1710–1711, or 171$\frac{0}{1}$, meaning 1710, if the reader observed March 25 as New Year's Day ; 1711 if he observed January 1.

because it was almost wholly the work of the two best writers of English of that time, Joseph Addison and Sir Richard Steele. Both of these men were artists in letters, but they had that wholesome view of life, also, which forbade them to treat men and manners merely as playthings for the imagination. The essay was the form of literature which they found most available, for it was the nearest artistic reproduction of social intercourse, and the London of the early part of the eighteenth century was the London of coffee-houses, of court manners extending into the multitude of families which allied themselves with the two great parties in English politics, and the London of a commercial class rising into dignity and power.

In the essay as Addison and Steele perfected it lay as yet undeveloped the modern novel. The romance was a form of literature recognized and accepted, and when the writers of these essays feigned narratives of distressed or inquiring damsels, they often gave them names out of the romances as Annabella, Eucratia, Amaryllis, Leonora, and the like. But they fell, also, into the way of calling the fictitious figures Patience Giddy, Thomas Trusty, Sam Hopewell, and similar homely names, and at every stroke came nearer, also, to the familiar forms of actual life. It is apparent that the popularity of the "Spectator" from the first was due largely to the reality with which its authors invested the characters whom they impersonated. As soon as the Spectator himself had drawn his own portrait, he enlisted the interest and attention of a compact society of readers in London who loved gossip and social intercourse and were delighted to see their taste thus reflected in graceful literature. And

when the next day this new paper proceeded to sketch
a group of individual men, making them, after the
fashion of the day, a club, the possibilities which
lay in this reproduction, as in a mirror, of contempo-
raneous society, were so great that men and women
everywhere received with enthusiasm this new creation in letters, and the projectors of the paper were
inspirited by their instantaneous success.

It cannot be said that either Addison or Steele
perceived the full force of what they had done. Their
main interest was still in criticism of life, and the
figures they so deftly manipulated were rather agreeable reliefs, and even occasional mouthpieces of senti-
ment, than living persons whose fortunes were of the
utmost importance. Still, there these creations were,
and from time to time the artists who fashioned them
revived them for their delight and added one touch
of nature after another. The central figure was that
of Sir Roger de Coverley, and the instinct of the artist
led Addison with Steele's fine assistance to extend
the fullest treatment upon the knight in his country
home, rather than in the town.

In pursuance of their purpose, the writers of the
"Spectator" introduced the various members of the
club frequently into the discussions which formed
the topics of the several papers. The club is always
more or less supposed. In separating, therefore, those
papers which may be grouped under the general head
of "The Sir Roger de Coverley Papers," there is room
for diverse judgment. It is easy enough to say that a
very large number of the "Spectator" papers should be
excluded, but the several editors who have undertaken
to make a consistent group, beginning with the ac-

complished W. Henry Wills, who set the example, all differ in their choice, though agreement will be found to hold for the majority of papers. Not every chapter in this book is exclusively concerned with Sir Roger, and there are several papers omitted in which his name occurs, but the selection is on the whole more inclusive than any that has hitherto been made. It should be observed that the titles given to the successive chapters do not occur in the "Spectator."

The first and chief object in reading a work in pure literature is the enjoyment of the art; the second, not far removed when the work belongs to another generation, is the aid which it furnishes the reader in vivifying his imagination of historic life. A novel like one of Fielding's goes much further in transporting one into the eighteenth century than a history of the manners and customs of that period like the serviceable one by Mr. Sydney.[1] The editor of this edition of "Sir Roger de Coverley," therefore, has aimed in his notes mainly to enrich the reader's mind in particulars where the text, though not obscure, may be illustrated. The more one can be put when reading into the familiar attitude of the first readers of these papers, the more completely will one live the book. At the same time it has not been thought worth while to check the reader's interest in answering for himself the questions which will arise. For this reason explanation has been avoided of words and terms which may be found in any comprehensive dictionary; such words, for example, as Whig, Tory,

---

1. *England and the English in the Eighteenth Century; Chapters in the Social History of the Times.* By WILLIAM CONNOR SYDNEY. In two volumes. London and New York: Macmillan & Co. 1891.

put, smoke, fagots in a regiment, quorum, need not long puzzle a student who has access to such a dictionary. Now and then curiosity has been appealed to in reference to variations in the English of the eighteenth century and that of to-day. It has not been thought necessary to give meagre facts and dates regarding the great historic names which occur in slight mention.

The text used is that furnished by Mr. Henry Morley in his convenient edition of the " Spectator,"[1] and for the interest of the student the last " speculation " is given exactly as first printed as regards spelling, capitalization, and italics. For the purpose of still further removing the reader from the present, it might have been desirable to print the entire book in this style; but a specimen only is given lest the unaccustomed reader should grow confused in his own usage.

The main incidents in the lives of Addison and Steele are given in the chronological table which follows, but the reader who desires to become more intimate with these persons should read Thackeray's "The English Humorists." The same great writer's novel of "Henry Esmond" will put him more fully in sympathy with the spirit of the eighteenth century.

1. *The Spectator.* A new edition, reproducing the original text both as first issued and as corrected by its authors. With Introduction, Notes, and Index, by HENRY MORLEY. In three volumes. London : George Routledge & Sons. 1883.

CHRONOLOGICAL TABLE OF THE LIVES OF
ADDISON, STEELE, AND BUDGELL.

JOSEPH ADDISON.

Born at Milston, near Amesbury, in Wiltshire, May 1, 1672.

Educated in schools at Amesbury, Salisbury, and Lichfield, to which last place the family removed when his father, the Rev. Lancelot Addison, became Dean of the Cathedral in 1683.

Thence he is sent to the Charterhouse School in London, where Steele was a scholar at the same time, and enters Queen's College, Oxford, in 1687.

Becomes Fellow of Magdalen College in 1698.

Receives a pension from the government, the Whig party being dominant, travels on the Continent to qualify himself for diplomatic service, and returns to England in 1703.

Publishes *Remarks on Several Parts of Italy*, 1705.

Appointed Under Secretary of State, 1706.

Elected Member of Parliament, 1708.

Contributes to Steele's paper, *The Tatler*, 1709.

Begins *The Spectator*, 1710–11.

Writes the tragedy of *Cato*, 1713.

Contributes to Steele's *The Guardian*, 1713.

Marries the Countess of Warwick, August 3, 1716.

Dies June 17, 1719.

RICHARD STEELE.

Born in Dublin, Ireland, son of an Irish attorney, March, 1671–72.

Is sent to the Charterhouse School, 1684.

Enters Christchurch, Oxford, March, 1690.

Leaves Oxford and enlists as a private soldier, 1694.

Becomes Captain Steele, 1700.

Writes and publishes *The Christian Hero*, 1701.

Produces on the stage *The Funeral, or Grief à la Mode*, 1701.

Marries Mrs. Margaret Stretch, a widow, spring of 1705.

Is made editor of the official *Gazette*, 1706.

Mrs. Steele dies, December, 1706.

Marries Mary Scurlock, September 9, 1707.

Publishes the first number of *The Tatler*, April 12, 1709.

Is made Commissioner of Stamps, January, 1710.

Writes for *The Spectator*, 1711–12.

Begins *The Guardian*, March 12, 1713.

Enters Parliament, 1713.

Becomes patentee of Drury Lane Theatre, 1715.

Is knighted by George I., 1715.

Produces his most successful comedy, *The Conscious Lovers*, 1722.

Dies at Carmarthen, September 1, 1729.

EUSTACE BUDGELL.

Born 1686, at St. Thomas, near Exeter, Eng.; a cousin of Addison.
Called to the bar, but through his connection with Addison takes up
literary work. Writes thirty-seven of the Spectator papers.
In 1733 starts " The Bee," which continues two years.
Through Addison's influence Budgell holds various public offices.
Becomes involved in disgraceful financial difficulties which affect his
mind.
Commits suicide in the Thames, 1736.

CRITICAL ESTIMATES.

Closing paragraphs from Dr. Samuel Johnson's Addison
in " Lives of the English Poets."

As a describer of life and manners Addison must be allowed to
stand perhaps the first of the first rank. His humor, which, as Steele
observes, is peculiar to himself, is so happily diffused as to give the
grace of novelty to domestic scenes and daily occurrences. He never
"outsteps the modesty of nature," nor raises merriment or wonder
by the violation of truth. His figures neither divert by distortion
nor amaze by aggravation. He copies life with so much fidelity
that he can hardly be said to invent; yet his exhibitions have an air
so much original that it is difficult to suppose them not merely the
product of imagination.

As a teacher of wisdom he may be confidently followed. His
religion has nothing in it enthusiastic or superstitious; he appears
neither weakly credulous nor wantonly sceptical; his morality is
neither dangerously lax nor impracticably rigid. All the enchant-
ment of fancy and all the cogency of argument are employed to
recommend to the reader his real interest, the care of pleasing the
Author of his being. Truth is shown sometimes as the phantom of a
vision; sometimes appears half-veiled in an allegory; sometimes at-
tracts regard in the robes of fancy; and sometimes steps forth in the
confidence of reason. She wears a thousand dresses, and in all is
pleasing.

> "Mille habet ornatus, mille decenter habet."

His prose is the model of the middle style; on grave subjects not formal, on light occasions not grovelling; pure without scrupulosity, and
exact without apparent elaboration; always equable and always easy,
without glowing words or pointed sentences. Addison never deviates
from his track to snatch a grace; he seeks no ambitious ornaments
and tries no hazardous innovations. His page is always luminous, but
never blazes in unexpected splendor.

It was apparently his principal endeavor to avoid all harshness and severity of diction ; he is therefore sometimes verbose in his transitions and connections, and sometimes descends too much to the language of conversation ; yet if his language had been less idiomatical it might have lost somewhat of its genuine Anglicism. What he attempted he performed ; he is never feeble, and he did not wish to be energetic ; he is never rapid and he never stagnates. His sentences have neither studied amplitude nor affected brevity ; his periods, though not diligently rounded, are voluble and easy. Whoever wishes to attain an English style, familiar but not coarse, and elegant but not ostentatious, must give his days and nights to the volumes of Addison.

From Macaulay's Essay on Addison.

"He is entitled to be considered, not only as the greatest of the English essayists, but as the forerunner of the great English novelists. . . . The great satirist, who alone knew how to use ridicule without abusing it, who without inflicting a wound effected a great social reform, and who reconciled wit and virtue, after a long and disastrous separation, during which wit had been led astray by profligacy, and virtue by fanaticism."

From Thackeray's English Humorists.

Addison wrote his papers as gayly as if he were going out for a holiday. When Steele's "Tatler" first began his prattle, Addison, then in Ireland, caught at his friend's notion, poured in paper after paper, and contributed the stores of his mind, the sweet fruits of his reading, the delightful gleanings of his daily observation, with a wonderful profusion, and as it seemed, an almost endless fecundity. He was six and thirty years old ; full and ripe. . . . He had not done much as yet. . . . But with his friend's discovery of the "Tatler," Addison's calling was found, and the most delightful talker in the world began to speak.

A VIEW OF THE CHARTERHOUSE. 1864

SIR ROGER DE COVERLEY.

Non fumum ex fulgore, sed ex fumo dare lucem
Cogitat, ut speciosa dehinc miracula promat.[1]
HORACE, *Ars Poetica*, 143, 144.

I HAVE observed that a reader seldom peruses a
book with pleasure 'till he knows whether the writer
of it be a black or a fair man, of a mild or choleric
disposition, married or a bachelor, with other particulars of the like nature, that conduce very much to
the right understanding of an author.[2] To gratify
this curiosity, which is so natural to a reader, I design
this paper and my next as prefatory discourses to my
following writings, and shall give some account in

1.   His thought it is, not smoke from flame,
       But out of smoke a steadfast light to bring,
       That in the light bright wonders he may frame.

2. In his *Notes on Walter Savage Landor*, De Quincey (iv.
407), commenting on this passage, says : " No reader cares about
an author's person before reading his book ; it is after reading
it, and supposing the book to reveal something of the writer's
moral nature, as modifying his intellect ; it is for his fun, his
fancy, his sadness, possibly his craziness, that any reader cares
about seeing the author in person. Afflicted with the very saty-
riasis of curiosity, no man ever wished to see the author of a
Ready Reckoner, or of the *Agistment Tithe*, or on the *Present
Deplorable Dry Rot in Potatoes.*"

them of the several[1] persons that are engaged in this work. As the chief trouble of compiling, digesting, and correcting, will fall to my share, I must do myself the justice to open the work with my own history.[2]

I was born to a small hereditary estate, which, according to the tradition of the village where it lies, was bounded by the same hedges and ditches in William the Conqueror's time that it is at present, and has been delivered down from father to son whole and entire,[3] without the loss or acquisition of a single field or meadow, during the space of six hundred years. There runs a story in the family, that [before I was born] my mother dreamt that she was [to bring forth] a judge; whether this might proceed from a lawsuit which was then depending in the family, or my father's being a justice of the peace, I cannot determine; for I am not so vain as to think it presaged any dignity that I should arrive at in my future life, though that was the interpretation which the neighborhood put upon it. The gravity of my behavior at my very first appearance in the world seemed to favor my mother's dream: for, as she has often told me, I threw away my rattle before I was two months old, and would not make use of my coral till they had taken away the bells from it.

1. Note that "several" is used in its specific meaning not of many, but of separate persons.

2. Addison is of course constructing an imaginary character and giving him a consistent history, but as Macaulay remarks in his essay on *The Life and Writings of Addison*, "It is not easy to doubt that the portrait was meant to be in some features a likeness of the painter." Especially may this be said of the humorously exaggerated characteristic of shyness.

3. Whole = with all its divisions ; entire = with each division perfect.

As for the rest of my infancy, there being nothing in it remarkable, I shall pass it over in silence. I find, that, during my nonage, I had the reputation of a very sullen youth, but was always a favorite of my schoolmaster, who used to say, *that my parts were solid, and would wear well.* I had not been long at the University, before I distinguished myself by a most profound silence; for, during the space of eight years, excepting in the public exercises of the college, I scarce uttered the quantity of an hundred words; and indeed do not remember that I ever spoke three sentences together in my whole life. Whilst I was in this learned body, I applied myself with so much diligence to my studies, that there are very few celebrated books, either in the learned or modern tongues, which I am not acquainted with.

Upon the death of my father, I was resolved to travel into foreign countries, and therefore left the University with the character of an odd unaccountable fellow, that had a great deal of learning, if I would but show it. An insatiable thirst after knowledge carried me into all the countries of Europe in which there was anything new or strange to be seen; nay, to such a degree was my curiosity raised, that having read the controversies [1] of some great men concerning the antiquities of Egypt, I made a voyage to Grand Cairo, on purpose to take the measure of a pyramid: and, as soon as I had set myself right in that particular, returned to my native country with great satisfaction.

1. In Addison's time, John Greaves, Professor of Astronomy at Oxford, had led in the discussion regarding the measurement of the pyramids, as in our day Piazzi Smyth, whose work, *Our Inheritance in the Great Pyramid*, still excites interest and debate.

I have passed my latter years in this city, where I am frequently seen in most public places, though there are not above half a dozen of my select friends that know me: of whom my next paper shall give a more particular account. There is no place of general resort wherein I do not often make my appearance; sometimes I am seen thrusting my head into a round of politicians at Will's,[1] and listening with great attention to the narratives that are made in those little circular audiences. Sometimes I smoke a pipe at Child's,[2] and while I seem attentive to nothing but the *Postman*,[3] overhear the conversation of every table in the room. I appear on Sunday nights at St. James's coffee-house,[4] and sometimes join the little committee of politics in the inner room,[5] as one who comes there to hear and improve. My face is likewise very well known at the Grecian,[6] the Cocoa Tree,[7] and in the theatres both of Drury Lane and

1. "The father of the modern club." Will's Coffee House stood on the northwest corner of Russell and Bow Streets, Covent Garden. It took its name from the proprietor, William Urwin, and derived its greatest reputation from the poet Dryden's resort to it.

2. In St. Paul's churchyard. From its neighborhood to the cathedral, Doctor's Commons, the College of Physicians, and the Royal Society, it was frequented by clergy, lawyers, physicians, and men of science.

3. *The Postman*, a journal edited by a French Protestant, M. Fonvive, was marked by the prominence it gave to foreign correspondence.

4. The headquarters of Whig politicians.

5. For a more particular account of what went on in the inner room, see *The Spectator*, No. 403.

6. So called from being kept by a Greek named Constantine. Its nearness to the Temple led to its being the rendezvous of men of learning.

7. The Tory headquarters.

the Hay Market. I have been taken for a merchant upon the Exchange for above these ten years, and sometimes pass for a Jew in the assembly of stock-jobbers at Jonathan's.[1] In short, wherever I see a cluster of people, I always mix with them, though I never open my lips but in my own club.

Thus I live in the world rather as a spectator of mankind than as one of the species; by which means I have made myself a speculative statesman, soldier, merchant, and artisan, without ever meddling with any practical part in life. I am very well versed in the theory of a husband or a father, and can discern the errors in the economy,[2] business, and diversion of others, better than those who are engaged in them: as standers-by discover blots,[3] which are apt to escape those who are in the game. I never espoused any party with violence, and am resolved to observe an exact neutrality between the Whigs and Tories, unless I shall be forced to declare myself by the hostilities of either side. In short, I have acted in all the parts of my life as a looker-on, which is the character I intend to preserve in this paper.

I have given the reader just so much of my history and character, as to let him see I am not altogether unqualified for the business I have undertaken. As for other particulars in my life and adventures, I shall insert them in following papers, as I shall see

1. Jonathan's coffee-house was the resort of the more questionable sort of stock-jobbers.

2. In *The Spectator* as originally printed, the spelling of this word œconomy emphasized its meaning as derived from the Greek, the "management of the house."

3. In the game of backgammon, "to make a blot" was to leave a piece exposed.

occasion. In the mean time, when I consider how much I have seen, read, and heard, I begin to blame my own taciturnity; and since I have neither time nor inclination to communicate the fulness of my heart in speech, I am resolved to do it in writing, and to print myself out, if possible, before I die. I have been often told by my friends, that it is pity so many useful discoveries which I have made should be in the possession of a silent man. For this reason, therefore, I shall publish a sheet full of thoughts every morning, for the benefit of my contemporaries; and if I can any way contribute to the diversion or improvement of the country in which I live, I shall leave it when I am summoned out of it, with the secret satisfaction of thinking that I have not lived in vain.

There are three very material points which I have not spoken to[1] in this paper, and which, for several important reasons, I must keep to myself, at least for some time: I mean, an account of my name, my age, and my lodgings. I must confess I would gratify my reader in anything that is reasonable; but as for these three particulars, though I am sensible they might tend very much to the embellishment of my paper, I cannot yet come to a resolution of communicating them to the public. They would indeed draw me out of that obscurity which I have enjoyed for many years, and expose me in public places to several salutes and civilities, which have been always very disagreeable to me; for the greatest pain I can suffer is the being talked to, and being stared at. It is for

---

1. This phrase lingers in forensic terms, and " he speaks to the point," though used now to express pertinence of speech, once had the meaning of the text.

this reason likewise that I keep my complexion and dress as very great secrets; though it is not impossible but I may make discoveries of both in the progress of the work I have undertaken.

After having been thus particular upon myself, I shall in to-morrow's paper give an account of those gentlemen who are concerned with me in this work; for, as I have before intimated, a plan of it is laid and concerted (as all other matters of importance are) in a club. However, as my friends have engaged me to stand in the front, those who have a mind to correspond with me may direct their letters to the SPECTATOR, at Mr. Buckley's in Little Britain.[1] For I must further acquaint the reader, that though our club meets only on Tuesdays and Thursdays, we have appointed a committee to sit every night, for the inspection of all such papers as may contribute to the advancement of the public weal.

II. THE CLUB.

Ast alii sex,
Et plures, uno conclamant ore.[2]
JUVENAL, *Satire* vii. 167.

THE first of our society is a gentleman of Worcestershire, of ancient descent, a baronet, his name Sir

---

1. In the *Daily Courant* of March 1, 1711, the first daily newspaper, published by Buckley, appeared this advertisement : "This day is published a Paper entitled THE SPECTATOR at the Dolphin, in Little Britain, and sold by A. Baldwin in Warwick Lane."

2. Six others at least,
And more, call out together with a single voice.

Roger de Coverley.[1] His great-grandfather was in-
ventor of that famous country-dance which is called
after him.[2] All who know that shire are very well
acquainted with the parts and merits of Sir Roger.
He is a gentleman that is very singular in his behavior, but his singularities proceed from his good sense,
and are contradictions to the manners of the world
only as he thinks the world is in the wrong. However, this humor creates him no enemies, for he does
nothing with sourness or obstinacy; and his being
unconfined to modes and forms makes him but the
readier and more capable to please and oblige all who
know him. When he is in town, he lives in Soho

1. It is an idle curiosity which seeks to identify the imaginary
characters of these papers with actual persons. Even if it could
be known to a certainty that this or that English knight or country gentleman sat for his portrait, the characters which bear the
names given by Steele and Addison are more real to us than the
obscure men who suggested them. But there is strong reason
for believing that the authors of these characters took particular
pains to avoid confounding them with known men. Steele had
once got himself into trouble by too close copies of living men,
and Addison in the last number of *The Spectator* for this year,
when the popularity of the several figures had set the gossips
discussing their origin, takes pains to say : "I have shown in
a former paper, with how much care I have avoided all such
thoughts as are loose, obscene, or immoral ; and I believe my
reader would still think the better of me, if he knew the pains
I am at in qualifying what I write after such a manner, that
nothing may be interpreted as aimed at private persons." In a
word, these writers did what every self-respecting novelist to-
day does ; they studied human nature, but respected the individual person.

2. It was a clever turn to name the principal character after
a popular dance of the day, and then gravely derive the dance
from an ancestor of the hero. Steele says he was indebted to
Swift for this.

Square.[1] It is said he keeps himself a bachelor by
reason he was crossed in love by a perverse beautiful
widow of the next county to him. Before this disappointment, Sir Roger was what you call a fine gentleman, had often supped with my Lord Rochester and
Sir George Etherege,[2] fought a duel upon his first
coming to town, and kicked Bully Dawson[3] in a public coffee-house for calling him "youngster." But
being ill used by the above mentioned widow, he was
very serious for a year and a half; and though, his
temper being naturally jovial, he at last got over it,
he grew careless of himself, and never dressed afterwards. He continues to wear a coat and doublet of
the same cut that were in fashion at the time of his
repulse, which, in his merry humors, he tells us, has
been in and out[4] twelve times since he first wore it.
He is now in his fifty-sixth year, cheerful, gay, and
hearty; keeps a good house in both town and country; a great lover of mankind; but there is such a

1. The square had been built upon about forty years previous,
but the district bearing the name had been so called as early as
1632. The origin of the name is referred conjecturally to the
cry used by hunters when calling off the dogs from the hare ; a
conjecture which is partly supported by the name Dogfields
applied to a neighboring spot. In the early part of the seventeenth century it was hunting-ground. It was still a fashionable
quarter in 1711, though Sir Roger's residence is referred to an
earlier period when its glory was less dimmed.

2. The Earl of Rochester and Sir George Etherege were wits
and courtiers in the dissolute times of Charles II.

3. Bully Dawson was a swaggerer of the time who copied the
morals but not the wit of the court, and belonged to a lower
social grade. As Rochester died in 1680 and Etherege in 1689,
it is allowable to guess that Sir Roger when resenting Bully
Dawson's contemptuous epithet was under twenty-five.

4. That is, of the fashion.

mirthful cast in his behavior, that he is rather beloved than esteemed.[1] His tenants grow rich, his servants look satisfied, all the young women profess love to him, and the young men are glad of his company: when he comes into a house he calls the servants by their names, and talks all the way up stairs to a visit. I must not omit that Sir Roger is a justice of the quorum; that he fills the chair at a quarter-session with great abilities; and, three months ago, gained universal applause by explaining a passage in the Game Act.[2]

The gentleman next in esteem and authority among us is another bachelor, who is a member of the Inner Temple;[3] a man of great probity, wit, and under-standing; but he has chosen his place of residence rather to obey the direction of an old humorsome father, than in pursuit of his own inclinations. He was placed there to study the laws of the land, and is the most learned of any of the house in those of the stage. Aristotle and Longinus are much better understood by him than Littleton or Coke.[4] The

1. The notion of "esteemed" as here used supposes a cold approval.

2. The Game Act ably expounded by Sir Roger was probably that of Charles II. which defined what persons were privileged to keep guns and bows and have hunting-grounds ; among these were landowners worth at least a hundred pounds a year, and the sons and heirs-apparent of esquires or of persons of higher degree.

3. There were four Inns of Court or societies of lawyers in London at this time, the Inner Temple, the Middle Temple, Lincoln's Inn, and Gray's Inn.

4. Aristotle, who lived three centuries before Christ, and Lon-ginus, who lived three centuries after Christ, were the classic ancient authorities on the criticism of art ; Littleton and Coke, the former in the fifteenth, and the latter who was a commen-

father sends up every post questions relating to mar-
riage-articles, leases, and tenures, in the neighborhood; all which questions he agrees with an attorney
to answer and take care of in the lump. He is study-
ing the passions themselves, when he should be inquiring into the debates among men which arise from
them. He knows the argument of each of the ora-
tions of Demosthenes and Tully,[1] but not one case in
the reports of our own courts. No one ever took him
for a fool, but none, except his intimate friends,
know he has a great deal of wit.[2] This turn makes
him at once both disinterested and agreeable: as few
of his thoughts are drawn from business, they are
most of them fit for conversation. His taste of books
is a little too just for the age he lives in; he has read
all, but approves of very few. His familiarity with
the customs, manners, actions, and writings of the
ancients makes him a very delicate observer of what
occurs to him in the present world. He is an excellent critic, and the time of the play is his hour of
business; exactly at five[3] he passes through New
Inn,[4] crosses through Russell Court, and takes a turn

tator on him, in the sixteenth, were the classic English authorities
on law.

1. Tully was for a long time the familiar mode in which
Marcus Tullius Cicero was spoken of in England.

2. It should be remembered that our limitation of the use of
this word did not prevail in the time of *The Spectator*, when its
more common significance as here was that of intellectual force.

3. In 1663 the theatrical performances began at three in the
afternoon. In 1667 the hour was four, and the time was gradually made later. In 1711 the hour was six, dinner having been
usually at three or four. The beau of the season after dinner
was wont to spend an hour at a coffee-house before the play.

4. There were pleasant walks and gardens attached to New
Inn, which was a precinct of Middle Temple.

at Will's till the play begins; he has his shoes rubbed
and his periwig powdered at the barber's as you go
into the Rose.[1] It is for the good of the audience
when he is at a play, for the actors have an ambition
to please him.

The person of next consideration is Sir Andrew
Freeport,[2] a merchant of great eminence in the city
of London, a person of indefatigable industry, strong
reason, and great experience. His notions of trade
are noble and generous, and (as every rich man has
usually some sly way of jesting, which would make
no great figure were he not a rich man) he calls the
sea the British Common. He is acquainted with
commerce in all its parts, and will tell you that it is
a stupid and barbarous way to extend dominion by
arms; for true power is to be got by arts and industry. He will often argue that if this part of our
trade were well cultivated, we should gain from one
nation; and if another, from another. I have heard
him prove that diligence makes more lasting acquisitions than valor, and that sloth has ruined more nations than the sword. He abounds in several frugal

1. The Rose Tavern in Covent Garden adjoining Drury Lane
Theatre was the haunt of dramatic authors.

2. From the character and opinions of Sir Andrew it is not
unlikely that in choosing his name Steele and Addison made allu-
sion to the policy then urged to abolish the commercial restric-
tions of the port of London. Dr. Johnson in his life of Addison
says: "To Sir Roger, who as a country gentleman appears to be
a Tory, or as it is generally expressed, an adherent to the landed
interest, is opposed Sir Andrew Freeport, a new man and a
wealthy merchant, zealous for the moneyed interest and a Whig.
Of this contrariety of opinions more consequences were at first
intended than could be produced when the resolution was taken
to exclude party from the paper."

maxims, amongst which the greatest favorite is, "A penny saved is a penny got." A general trader of good sense is pleasanter company than a general scholar; and Sir Andrew having a natural unaffected eloquence, the perspicuity of his discourse gives the same pleasure that wit would in another man. He has made his fortunes himself, and says that England may be richer than other kingdoms by as plain methods as he himself is richer than other men; though at the same time I can say this of him, that there is not a point in the compass but blows home a ship in which he is an owner.

Next to Sir Andrew in the club-room sits Captain Sentry, a gentleman of great courage, good understanding, but invincible modesty. He is one of those that deserve very well, but are very awkward at putting their talents within the observation of such as should take notice of them. He was some years a captain, and behaved himself with great gallantry in several engagements and at several sieges; but having a small estate of his own, and being next heir to Sir Roger,[1] he has quitted a way of life in which no man can rise suitably to his merit who is not something of a courtier as well as a soldier. I have heard him often lament that in a profession where merit is placed in so conspicuous a view, impudence should get the better of modesty. When he has talked to this purpose I never heard him make a sour expression, but frankly confess that he left the world because he was not fit for it. A strict honesty and an even regular behavior are in themselves obstacles to him that must press through crowds, who endeavor

1. In the last of these papers, Captain Sentry is further noted as nephew to Sir Roger.

at the same end with himself, — the favor of a com-
mander. He will, however, in this way of talk excuse
generals for not disposing according to men's desert,
or inquiring into it: "for," says he, "that great man
who has a mind to help me, has as many to break
through to come at me, as I have to come at him;"
therefore he will conclude, that the man who would
make a figure, especially in a military way, must get
over all false modesty, and assist his patron against
the importunity of other pretenders by a proper assurance in his own vindication. He says it is a civil
cowardice to be backward in asserting what you
ought to expect, as it is a military fear to be slow in
attacking when it is your duty. With this candor
does the gentleman speak of himself and others.
The same frankness runs through all his conversation.
The military part of his life has furnished him with
many adventures, in the relation of which he is very
agreeable to the company; for he is never overbear-
ing, though accustomed to command men in the
utmost degree below him; nor ever too obsequious
from a habit of obeying men highly above him.

But that our society may not appear a set of humorists [1] unacquainted with the gallantries and pleasures of the age, we have among us the gallant Will
Honeycomb, a gentleman who according to his years
should be in the decline of his life, but having ever
been very careful of his person, and always had a
very easy fortune, time has made but very little
impression either by wrinkles on his forehead, or

---

1. That is, persons who conduct themselves after their own
whims rather than by the conventional laws of society. Ben
Jonson emphasizes this significance of the word in his plays
Every Man in his Humor and *Every Man out of his Humor.*

traces in his brain. His person is well turned, and
of good height. He is very ready at that sort of
discourse with which men usually entertain women.
He has all his life dressed very well, and remembers
habits [1] as others do men. He can smile when one
speaks to him, and laughs easily. He knows the history of every mode, and can inform you from which
of the French king's wenches our wives and daughters had this manner of curling their hair, that way
of placing their hoods; whose frailty was covered by
such a sort of petticoat, and whose vanity to show
her foot made that part of the dress so short in such
a year; in a word, all his conversation and knowledge
has been in the female world. As other men of his
age will take notice to you what such a minister said
upon such and such an occasion, he will tell you
when the Duke of Monmouth [2] danced at court such
a woman was then smitten, another was taken with
him at the head of his troop in the Park. In all
these important relations, he has ever about the same
time received a kind glance or a blow of a fan from
some celebrated beauty, mother of the present Lord
Such-a-one. If you speak of a young commoner that
said a lively thing in the House, he starts up: "He
has good blood in his veins; Tom Mirabel begot him; [3]
the rogue cheated me in that affair: that young fel-

1. That is, dresses and costumes. We retain this use in the
compound riding-habit.
2. The handsome, dashing, and favorite son of Charles II.
"The queen . . . it seems, was at Windsor at the late St.
George's feast there, and the Duke of Monmouth dancing with
her with his hat in his hand, the king came in and kissed him,
and made him put on his hat, which everybody took notice of."
Pepys's Diary, April 27, 1663.
3. Mirabel was a favorite name in the comedies of the day.

low's mother used me more like a dog than any woman I ever made advances to." This way of talking of his very much enlivens the conversation among us of a more sedate turn; and I find there is not one of the company, but myself, who rarely speak at all, but speaks of him as of that sort of man who is usually called a well-bred fine gentleman. To conclude his character, where women are not concerned, he is an honest worthy man.

I cannot tell whether I am to account him whom I am next to speak of as one of our company, for he visits us but seldom; but when he does, it adds to every man else a new enjoyment of himself. He is a clergyman, a very philosophic man, of general learning, great sanctity of life, and the most exact good breeding. He has the misfortune to be of a very weak constitution, and consequently cannot accept of such cares and business as preferments in his function would oblige him to; he is therefore among divines what a chamber-counsellor is among lawyers. The probity of his mind, and the integrity of his life, create him followers, as being eloquent or loud advances others. He seldom introduces the subject he speaks upon; but we are so far gone in years, that he observes, when he is among us, an earnestness to have him fall on some divine topic, which he always treats with much authority, as one who has no interests in this world, as one who is hastening to the object of all his wishes, and conceives hope from his decays and infirmities. These are my ordinary companions.

III. SIR ROGER ON MEN OF FINE PARTS.

Credebant hoc grande nefas, et morte piandum,
Si juvenis vetulo non assurrexerat.[1]
JUVENAL, *Satire* xiii. 54, 55.

I KNOW no evil under the sun so great as the abuse of the understanding, and yet there is no one vice more common. It has diffused itself through both sexes, and all qualities of mankind; and there is hardly that person to be found, who is not more concerned for the reputation of wit and sense, than honesty and virtue. But this unhappy affectation of being wise rather than honest, witty than good-natured, is the source of most of the ill habits of life. Such false impressions are owing to the abandoned writings of men of wit, and the awkward imitation of the rest of mankind.

For this reason Sir Roger was saying last night, that he was of opinion that none but men of fine parts deserve to be hanged. The reflections of such men are so delicate upon all occurrences which they are concerned in, that they should be exposed to more than ordinary infamy and punishment, for offending against such quick admonitions as their own souls give them, and blunting the fine edge of their minds in such a manner, that they are no more shocked at vice and folly than men of slower capacities. There is no greater monster in being than a very ill man of great parts. He lives like a man in a palsy, with one side of him dead. While perhaps he enjoys the satisfaction of luxury, of wealth, of ambition, he has lost the taste of good-will, of friend-

1.   They held it impious and a capital crime
      If a youth did not rise in the presence of age.

ship, of innocence. Scarecrow, the beggar, in Lincoln's-inn-fields,[1] who disabled himself in his right leg, and asks alms all day to get himself a warm supper and a trull at night, is not half so despicable a wretch, as such a man of sense. The beggar has no relish above sensations; he finds rest more agreeable than motion; and while he has a warm fire and his doxy, never reflects that he deserves to be whipped. Every man who terminates his satisfaction and enjoyments within the supply of his own necessities and passions is, says Sir Roger, in my eye, as poor a rogue as Scarecrow. "But," continued he, "for the loss of public and private virtue, we are beholden to your men of parts forsooth; it is with them no matter what is done, so it is done with an air. But to me, who am so whimsical in a corrupt age as to act according to nature and reason, a selfish man, in the most shining circumstance and equipage, appears in the same condition with the fellow above-mentioned, but more contemptible in proportion to what more he robs the public of, and enjoys above him. I lay it down therefore for a rule, that the whole man is to move together; that every action of any importance is to have a prospect of public good; and that the general tendency of our indifferent actions ought to be agreeable to the dictates of reason, of religion, of good-breeding; without this, a man, as I have before hinted, is hopping instead of walking, he is not in his entire and proper motion."

1. A public square in the immediate vicinity, as its name indicates, of Lincoln's Inn. "These celebrated fields," says Peter Cunningham in his *Handbook of London*, "were frequented from a very early period down to the year 1735 by wrestlers, bowlers, cripples, beggars, and idle boys."

While the honest knight was thus bewildering himself in good starts, I looked attentively upon him, which made him, I thought, collect his mind a little. "What I aim at," says he, "is to represent that I am of opinion, to polish our understandings, and neglect our manners, is of all things the most inexcusable. Reason should govern passion, but instead of that, you see, it is often subservient to it; and, as unaccountable as one would think it, a wise man is not always a good man." This degeneracy is not only the guilt of particular persons, but also, at some times, of a whole people; and perhaps it may appear upon examination, that the most polite ages are the least virtuous. This may be attributed to the folly of admitting wit and learning as merit in themselves, without considering the application of them. By this means it becomes a rule, not so much to regard what we do, as how we do it. But this false beauty will not pass upon men of honest minds and true taste. Sir Richard Blackmore [1] says, with as much good sense as virtue, "It is a mighty dishonor and shame to employ excellent faculties and abundance of wit, to humor and please men in their vices and follies. The great enemy of mankind, notwithstanding his wit and angelic faculties, is the most odious being in the whole creation." He goes on soon after to say, very generously, that he undertook the writing of his poem "to rescue the Muses out of the hands

1. Blackmore was born in 1650 and had at this time printed a number of dull poems. He was a physician, esteemed for his good sense and virtue, but his character, though it made his contemporaries respect him and extend their civility to his writings, has not preserved those writings in the interest of posterity. The passage here quoted is said to be a condensation of a manuscript unpublished at the time.

of ravishers, to restore them to their sweet and chaste mansions, and to engage them in an employment suitable to their dignity." This certainly ought to be the purpose of every man who appears in public, and whoever does not proceed upon that foundation injures his country as fast as he succeeds in his studies. When modesty ceases to be the chief ornament of one sex, and integrity of the other, society is upon a wrong basis, and we shall be ever after without rules to guide our judgment in what is really becoming and ornamental. Nature and reason direct one thing, passion and humor another. To follow the dictates of the two latter is going into a road that is both endless and intricate; when we pursue the other, our passage is delightful, and what we aim at easily attainable.

I do not doubt but England is at present as polite a nation as any in the world; but any man who thinks can easily see, that the affectation of being gay and in fashion has very near eaten up our good sense and our religion. Is there anything so just as that mode and gallantry should be built upon exerting ourselves in what is proper and agreeable to the institutions of justice and piety among us? And yet is there anything more common than that we run in perfect contradiction to them? All which is supported by no other pretension than that it is done with what we call a good grace.

Nothing ought to be held laudable or becoming, but what nature itself should prompt us to think so. Respect to all kinds of superiors is founded methinks upon instinct; and yet what is so ridiculous as age? I make this abrupt transition to the mention of this vice, more than any other, in order to introduce a

little story, which I think a pretty instance that the
most polite age is in danger of being the most
vicious.

"It happened at Athens, during a public represen-
tation of some play exhibited in honor of the commonwealth, that an old gentleman came too late for
a place suitable to his age and quality. Many of the
young gentlemen, who observed the difficulty and
confusion he was in, made signs to him that they
would accommodate him if he came where they sat.
The good man bustled through the crowd accordingly; but when he came to the seats to which he was
invited, the jest was to sit close and expose him, as
he stood, out of countenance, to the whole audience.
The frolic went round all the Athenian benches. But
on those occasions there were also particular places
assigned for foreigners. When the good man
skulked towards the boxes appointed for the Lacedæmonians, that honest people, more virtuous than
polite, rose up all to a man, and with the greatest
respect received him among them. The Athenians
being suddenly touched with a sense of the Spartan
virtue and their own degeneracy, gave a thunder of
applause; and the old man cried out, ' The Athenians understand what is good, but the Lacedæmonians
practise it.' " [1]

1. This paper has little directly to do with Sir Roger. Indeed, his name is quite all that connects him with its sentiments.
The quotation marks follow the original, but it is not easy to
say when the Spectator and when Sir Roger is speaking. It
suggests that the first design of Addison and Steele was not so
much to build up a character as to furnish convenient stalking
horses for such opinions as they might deliver, and the next
paper seems to confirm this view.

IV. A MEETING OF THE CLUB.

Parcit
Cognatis maculis similis fera.[1]
JUVENAL, *Satires*, 159.

THE club of which I am a member is very luckily
composed of such persons as are engaged in different
ways of life, and deputed as it were out of the most
conspicuous classes of mankind: by this means I am
furnished with the greatest variety of hints and materials, and know everything that passes in the different quarters and divisions, not only of this great city,
but of the whole kingdom. My readers, too, have
the satisfaction to find, that there is no rank or
degree among them who have not their representative
in this club, and that there is always somebody present who will take care of their respective interests,
that nothing may be written or published to the prejudice or infringement of their just rights and privileges.

I last night sat very late in company with this
select body of friends, who entertained me with several remarks which they and others had made upon
these my speculations, as also with the various success, which they had met with among their several
ranks and degrees of readers. Will Honeycomb
told me, in the softest manner he could, that there
were some ladies (but for your comfort, says Will,
they are not those of the most wit) that were offended
at the liberties I had taken with the opera and the
puppet-show;[2] that some of them were likewise very

1. The wild beast spares the creature marked like itself.
2. In a number of *The Spectator* the previous week.

much surprised, that I should think such serious points as the dress and equipage of persons of quality proper subjects for raillery.[1]

He was going on, when Sir Andrew Freeport took him up short, and told him, that the papers he hinted at had done great good in the city, and that all their wives and daughters were the better for them: and further added, that the whole city thought themselves very much obliged to me for declaring my generous intentions to scourge vice and folly as they appear in a multitude, without condescending to be a publisher of particular intrigues and cuckoldoms. In short, says Sir Andrew, if you avoid that foolish beaten road of falling upon aldermen and citizens, and employ your pen upon the vanity and luxury of courts, your paper must needs be of general use.

Upon this my friend the Templar told Sir Andrew, that he wondered to hear a man of his sense talk after that manner; that the city had always been the province for satire; and that the wits of king Charles's time jested upon nothing else during his whole reign. He then showed, by the examples of Horace, Juvenal, Boileau, and the best writers of every age, that the follies of the stage and court had never been accounted too sacred for ridicule, how great soever the persons might be that patronized them. But after all, says he, I think your raillery has made too great an excursion, in attacking several persons of the inns of court; and I do not believe you can show me any precedent for your behavior in that particular.

My good friend Sir Roger de Coverley, who had said nothing all this while, began his speech with a

1. As, for example, in Number Sixteen.

pish! and told us, that he wondered to see so many men of sense so very serious upon fooleries. "Let our good friend," says he, "attack every one that deserves it; I would only advise you, Mr. Spectator," applying himself to me, "to take care how you meddle with country squires: they are the ornaments of the English nation; men of good heads and sound bodies! and let me tell you, some of them take it ill of you, that you mention foxhunters with so little respect."

Captain Sentry spoke very sparingly on this occasion. What he said was only to commend my prudence in not touching upon the army, and advised me to continue to act discreetly in that point.

By this time I found every subject of my speculations was taken away from me, by one or other of the club; and began to think myself in the condition of the good man that had one wife who took a dislike to his gray hairs, and another to his black, till by their picking out what each of them had an aversion to, they left his head altogether bald and naked.

While I was thus musing with myself, my worthy friend the clergyman, who, very luckily for me, was at the club that night, undertook my cause. He told us, that he wondered any order of persons should think themselves too considerable to be advised: that it was not quality, but innocence, which exempted men from reproof: that vice and folly ought to be attacked wherever they could be met with, and especially when they were placed in high and conspicuous stations of life. He further added, that my paper would only serve to aggravate the pains of poverty, if it chiefly exposed those who are already depressed, and in some measure turned into ridicule, by the meanness of their conditions and circumstances. He

afterwards proceeded to take notice of the great use
this paper might be of to the public, by reprehending
those vices which are too trivial for the chastisement
of the law, and too fantastical for the cognizance of
the pulpit. He then advised me to prosecute my
undertaking with cheerfulness, and assured me, that
whoever might be displeased with me, I should be
approved by all those whose praises do honor to the
persons on whom they are bestowed.

The whole club pays a particular deference to the
discourse of this gentleman, and are drawn into what
he says, as much by the candid and ingenuous manner with which he delivers himself, as by the strength
of argument and force of reason which he makes use
of. Will Honeycomb immediately agreed that what
he had said was right; and that for his part, he would
not insist upon the quarter which he had demanded
for the ladies. Sir Andrew gave up the city with the
same frankness. The Templar would not stand out:
and was followed by Sir Roger and the Captain: who
all agreed that I should be at liberty to carry the war
into what quarter I pleased; provided I continued to
combat with criminals in a body, and to assault the
vice without hurting the person.

This debate, which was held for the good of mankind, put me in mind of that which the Roman tri-
umvirate were formerly engaged in, for their destruction. Every man at first stood hard for his friend,
till they found that by this means they should spoil
their proscription: and at length, making a sacrifice
of all their acquaintance and relations, furnished out
a very decent execution.

Having thus taken my resolution to march on
boldly in the cause of virtue and good sense, and to

annoy their adversaries in whatever degree or rank of men they may be found, I shall be deaf for the future to all the remonstrances that shall be made to me on this account. If Punch grow extravagant, I shall reprimand him very freely: if the stage becomes a nursery of folly and impertinence, I shall not be afraid to animadvert upon it. In short, if I meet with anything in city, court, or country, that shocks modesty or good manners, I shall use my utmost endeavors to make an example of it. I must, however, intreat every particular person, who does me the honor to be a reader of this paper, never to think himself, or any one of his friends or enemies, aimed at in what is said: for I promise him, never to draw a faulty character which does not fit at least a thousand people; or to publish a single paper that is not written in the spirit of benevolence, and with a love to mankind.

V. LEONORA'S LIBRARY.

Non illa colo calathisve Minervæ
Fœmineas assueta manus.[1]
VIRGIL, *Æneid*, vii. 805, 806.

SOME months ago, my friend Sir Roger, being in the country, inclosed a letter to me, directed to a certain lady, whom I shall here call by the name of Leonora, and, as it contained matters of consequence, desired me to deliver it to her with my own hand. Accordingly I waited upon her ladyship pretty early in the morning, and was desired by her woman to walk into her lady's library, till such time as she was in a readiness to receive me. The very sound of a

1. Unbred to spinning, in the loom unskilled. — DRYDEN.

Lady's Library gave me a great curiosity to see it;
and, as it was some time before the lady came to me,
I had an opportunity of turning over a great many
of her books, which were ranged together in a very
beautiful order. At the end of the folios (which
were finely bound and gilt) were great jars of china
placed one above another in a very noble piece of
architecture. The quartos were separated from the
octavos by a pile of smaller vessels, which rose in a
delightful pyramid. The octavos were bounded by
tea-dishes of all shapes, colors, and sizes, which were
so disposed on a wooden frame that they looked like
one continued pillar indented with the finest strokes
of sculpture, and stained with the greatest variety
of dyes. That part of the library which was designed
for the reception of plays and pamphlets, and other
loose papers, was inclosed in a kind of square, consisting of one of the prettiest grotesque works that
ever I saw, and made up of scaramouches, lions,
monkeys, mandarins, trees, shells, and a thousand
other odd figures in China ware. In the midst of
the room was a little Japan table, with a quire of gilt
paper upon it, and on the paper a silver snuff-box
made in the shape of a little book. I found there
were several other counterfeit books upon the upper
shelves, which were carved in wood, and served only
to fill up the number, like fagots in the muster of
a regiment. I was wonderfully pleased with such a
mixt kind of furniture, as seemed very suitable both
to the lady and the scholar, and did not know at first
whether I should fancy myself in a grotto, or in a
library.

Upon my looking into the books, I found there
were some few which the lady had bought for her

own use, but that most of them had been got together, either because she had heard them praised, or because she had seen the authors of them. Among several that I examined, I very well remember these that follow.

Ogilby's Virgil.

Dryden's Juvenal.

Cassandra.

Cleopatra.[1]

Astræa.[2]

Sir Isaac Newton's Works.

The Grand Cyrus;[3] with a pin stuck in one of the middle leaves.

Pembroke's Arcadia.[4]

Locke of Human Understanding; with a paper of patches in it.

A spelling-book.

A Dictionary for the explanation of hard words.

Sherlock upon Death.

The fifteen Comforts of Matrimony.

Sir William Temple's Essays.

Father Malbranche's Search after Truth, translated into English.

A book of Novels.

1. *Cassandra* and *Cleopatra* were French romances which had been translated into English.

2. A pastoral romance translated from the French.

3. By Mademoiselle de Scudéri, the most popular writer of French romances of the day.

4. There was a superficial similarity between Pembroke's *Arcadia* and *Astræa* ; but for the most part, as the reader will notice, Leonora's reading of romances was confined to the French, since the English had hardly yet occupied the great field of fiction. It was thirty years before *Pamela* and *Joseph Andrews* appeared.

The Academy of Compliments.

Culpepper's Midwifery.

The Ladies' Calling.

Tales in Verse by Mr. Durfey:[1] bound in red leather, gilt on the back, and doubled down in several places.

All the Classic Authors, in wood.

A set of Elzevers, by the same hand.

Clelia:[2] which opened of itself in the place that describes two lovers in a bower.

Baker's Chronicle.

Advice to a Daughter.

The new Atlantis, with a Key to it.[3]

Mr. Steele's Christian Hero.[4]

A Prayer-book; with a bottle of Hungary water by the side of it.

Dr. Sacheverell's Speech.[5]

Fielding's Trial.

Seneca's Morals.

Taylor's holy Living and Dying.

1. Thomas D'Urfey was a writer of somewhat free plays and songs, and a familiar companion of Charles II.

2. *Clelia* was another of Madame de Scudéri's romances.

3. A scandalous book whose full title was *Secret Memoirs and Manners of several Persons of Quality of both Sexes from the New Atlantis, an Island in the Mediterranean.* Under feigned names it slandered members of Whig families. It was a new book when Addison was writing, for it came out in 1709.

4. *The Christian Hero* was a serious work by Richard Steele, and was introduced apparently by Addison as a sly aside at his comrade in letters.

5. Dr. Henry Sacheverell was a clergyman who had just been lifted into prominence by an action foolishly brought against him by the Whigs for preaching two sermons obnoxious to them. The affair had much to do with the downfall of the Whig ministry.

La Ferte's Instructions for Country Dances.[1]

I was taking a catalogue in my pocket-book of these, and several other authors, when Leonora entered, and, upon my presenting her with the letter from the Knight, told me, with an unspeakable grace, that she hoped Sir Roger was in good health. I answered *yes;* for I hate long speeches, and after a bow or two retired.

Leonora was formerly a celebrated beauty, and is still a very lovely woman. She has been a widow for two or three years, and being unfortunate in her first marriage, has taken a resolution never to venture upon a second. She has no children to take care of, and leaves the management of her estate to my good friend Sir Roger. But as the mind naturally sinks into a kind of lethargy, and falls asleep, that is not agitated by some favorite pleasures and pursuits, Leonora has turned all the passions of her sex into a love of books and retirement. She converses chiefly with men, (as she has often said herself,) but it is only in their writings; and she admits of very few male-visitants, except my friend Sir Roger, whom she hears with great pleasure, and without scandal. As her reading has lain very much among romances, it has given her a very particular turn of thinking, and discovers itself even in her house, her gardens, and her furniture. Sir Roger has entertained me an hour together with a description of her country-seat, which is situated in a kind of wilderness, about an hundred miles distant from London, and looks like a little

1. La Ferte was the fashionable dancing-master of the day. It is not difficult to see in this jumble which were the books bought for Leonora for show and which she had chosen for her own delectation.

enchanted palace. The rocks about her are shaped
into artificial grottoes, covered with wood-bines and
jessamines. The woods are cut into shady walks,
twisted into bowers, and filled with cages of turtles.
The springs are made to run among pebbles, and by
that means taught to murmur very agreeably. They
are likewise collected into a beautiful lake, that is inhabited by a couple of swans, and empties itself by a
little rivulet which runs through a green meadow,
and is known in the family by the name of The Purl-
ing Stream. The Knight likewise tells me, that this
lady preserves her game better than any of the gentlemen in the country. "Not (says Sir Roger) that
she sets so great a value upon her partridges and
pheasants, as upon her larks and nightingales. For
she says that every bird which is killed in her ground
will spoil a consort, and that she shall certainly miss
him the next year."

When I think how oddly this lady is improved by
learning, I look upon her with a mixture of admiration and pity. Amidst these innocent entertainments
which she has formed to herself, how much more valuable does she appear than those of her sex, who
employ themselves in diversions that are less reasonable, though more in fashion! What improvements
would a woman have made, who is so susceptible of
impressions from what she reads, had she been guided
to such books as have a tendency to enlighten the
understanding and rectify the passions, as well as to
those which are of little more use than to divert the
imagination!

But the manner of a lady's employing herself use-
fully in reading shall be the subject of another paper,
in which I design to recommend such particular books

as may be proper for the improvement of the sex. And as this is a subject of a very nice nature, I shall desire my correspondents to give me their thoughts upon it.

VI. SIR ROGER AT HIS COUNTRY HOUSE.

Hinc tibi copia
Manabit ad plenum, benigno
Ruris honorum opulenta cornu.[1]
HORACE, *Odes,* I. xvii. 14–17.

HAVING often received an invitation from my friend Sir Roger de Coverley [2] to pass away a month with him in the country, I last week accompanied him thither, and am settled with him for some time at his country house, where I intend to form several of my ensuing speculations. Sir Roger, who is very well acquainted with my humor, lets me rise and go to bed when I please, dine at his own table or in my

1. [The Gods are my guardians, the Gods like my piety,
   And are pleased with my Muse ;] from their bounty shall
       flow
   For your use all the fruits of the earth to satiety,
   All the pleasures that Nature alone can bestow.
                                   John O. Sargent's translation.

2. It will be observed that it is four months since the introduction of the figure of Sir Roger, and the papers that intervene scarcely do anything toward filling out the character, so skillfully outlined by Steele. Indeed, of all the persons named in the second paper, Will Honeycomb is by far the most frequently named ; but it must not be inferred that Sir Roger had been out of mind. In the number for April 23d, Addison publishes a paper of Minutes for articles which the Spectator is supposed to have dropped accidentally in a coffee-house. The first memorandum is "Sir Roger de Coverley's Country Seat." He now takes up the character in good earnest, and with occasional help from Steele and Budgell makes it his own.

chamber as I think fit, sit still and say nothing without bidding me be merry. When the gentlemen of the country come to see him, he only shows me at a distance: as I have been walking in his fields I have observed them stealing a sight of me over an hedge,[1] and have heard the Knight desiring them not to let me see them, for that I hated to be stared at.

I am the more at ease in Sir Roger's family, because it consists of sober and staid persons; for, as the Knight is the best master in the world, he seldom changes his servants; and as he is beloved by all about him, his servants never care for leaving him; by this means his domestics are all in years, and grown old with their master. You would take his valet de chambre for his brother, his butler is gray-headed, his groom is one of the gravest men that I have ever seen, and his coachman has the looks of a privy counsellor. You see the goodness of the master even in the old house dog, and in a gray pad that is kept in the stable with great care and tenderness, out of regard to his past services, though he has been useless for several years.

I could not but observe with a great deal of pleasure, the joy that appeared in the countenances of these ancient domestics upon my friend's arrival at his country-seat. Some of them could not refrain from tears at the sight of their old master; every one of them pressed forward to do something for him, and seemed discouraged if they were not employed. At the same time the good old Knight, with the mixture of the father and the master of the family, tempered the inquiries after his own affairs with several kind

1. In Addison's time the distinction had not become fixed which uses *an* only before a vowel or silent *h.*

questions relating to themselves. This humanity and good-nature engages everybody to him, so that when he is pleasant[1] upon any of them, all his family are in good humor, and none so much as the person whom he diverts himself with: on the contrary, if he coughs, or betrays any infirmity of old age, it is easy for a stander-by to observe a secret concern in the looks of all his servants.

My worthy friend has put me under the particular care of his butler, who is a very prudent man, and, as well as the rest of his fellow-servants, wonderfully desirous of pleasing me, because they have often heard their master talk of me as of his particular friend.

My chief companion, when Sir Roger is diverting himself in the woods or the fields, is a very venerable man who is ever with Sir Roger, and has lived at his house in the nature of a chaplain above thirty years. This gentleman is a person of good sense and some learning, of a very regular life and obliging conversation: he heartily loves Sir Roger, and knows that he is very much in the old Knight's esteem, so that he lives in the family rather as a relation than a dependent.[2]

I have observed in several of my papers that my friend Sir Roger, amidst all his good qualities, is something of an humorist; and that his virtues as well as imperfections are, as it were, tinged by a certain extravagance, which makes them particularly

1. This sense of the word survives in the form *pleasantry.*
2. The literature of Addison's time is full of intimations of the inferior position of the country clergy. Fifty years later Goldsmith's *Vicar of Wakefield* gave evidence of the same social condition.

his, and distinguishes them from those of other men.
This cast of mind, as it is generally very innocent in
itself, so it renders his conversation highly agreeable,
and more delightful than the same degree of sense
and virtue would appear in their common and ordinary colors.   As I was walking with him last night,
he asked me how I liked the good man whom I have
just now mentioned, and without staying for my
answer told me that he was afraid of being insulted
with Latin and Greek at his own table, for which
reason he desired a particular friend of his at the
University to find him out a clergyman rather of
plain sense than much learning, of a good aspect, a
clear voice, a sociable temper, and, if possible, a
man that understood a little of backgammon.   My
friend, says Sir Roger, found me out this gentleman,
who, besides the endowments required of him, is,
they tell me, a good scholar, though he does not show
it: I have given him the parsonage of the parish;
and, because I know his value, have settled upon
him a good annuity for life.   If he outlives me, he
shall find that he was higher in my esteem than perhaps he thinks he is.   He has now been with me
thirty years, and, though he does not know I have
taken notice of it, has never in all that time asked
anything of me for himself, though he is every day
soliciting me for something in behalf of one or other
of my tenants his parishioners.   There has not been
a lawsuit in the parish since he has lived among
them: if any dispute arises they apply themselves to
him for the decision; if they do not acquiesce in
his judgment, which I think never happened above
once or twice at most, they appeal to me.   At his
first settling with me I made him a present of all the

good sermons which have been printed in English, and only begged of him that every Sunday he would pronounce one of them in the pulpit. Accordingly he has digested them into such a series, that they follow one another naturally, and make a continued system of practical divinity.

As Sir Roger was going on in his story, the gentleman we were talking of came up to us; and upon the Knight's asking him who preached to-morrow (for it was Saturday night) told us the Bishop of St. Asaph [1] in the morning, and Dr. South in the afternoon. He then showed us his list of preachers for the whole year, where I saw with a great deal of pleasure Archbishop Tillotson, Bishop Saunderson, Dr. Barrow, Dr. Calamy, with several living authors who have published discourses of practical divinity. I no sooner saw this venerable man in the pulpit, but I very much approved of my friend's insisting upon the qualifications of a good aspect and a clear voice; for I was so charmed with the gracefulness of his figure and delivery, as well as with the discourses he pronounced, that I think I never passed any time more to my satisfaction. A sermon repeated after this manner is like the composition of a poet in the mouth of a graceful actor.

I could heartily wish that more of our country clergy would follow this example; and, instead of wasting their spirits in laborious compositions of their own, would endeavor after a handsome elocution, and all those other talents that are proper to

1. William Beveridge, who had recently died, and whose sermons had a high popularity. It is possible, however, that Addison had in mind Dr. William Fleetwood who succeeded Beveridge.

enforce what has been penned by greater masters. This would not only be more easy to themselves, but more edifying to the people.

VII. THE COVERLEY HOUSEHOLD.

Æsopo ingentem statuam posuere Attici,
Servumque collocârunt æterna in basi,
Patere honoris scirent ut cuncti viam.[1]

PHÆDRUS, *Ep.* i. 2.

THE reception, manner of attendance, undisturbed freedom, and quiet, which I meet with here in the country, has confirmed me in the opinion I always had, that the general corruption of manners in servants is owing to the conduct of masters. The aspect of every one in the family carries so much satisfaction that it appears he knows the happy lot which has befallen him in being a member of it. There is one particular which I have seldom seen but at Sir Roger's; it is usual in all other places, that servants fly from the parts of the house through which their master is passing: on the contrary, here they industriously place themselves in his way; and it is on both sides, as it were, understood as a visit, when the servants appear without calling. This proceeds from the humane and equal temper of the man of the house, who also perfectly well knows how to enjoy a great estate with such economy as ever to be much beforehand. This makes his own mind untroubled, and consequently unapt to vent peevish expressions,

1. To Æsop a more than life-size statue did the Athenians raise.
   Slave though he was, they placed him on a solid base,
   That all might know how open lay the path of honor.

or give passionate or inconsistent orders to those about him. Thus respect and love go together, and a certain cheerfulness in performance of their duty is the particular distinction of the lower part of this family. When a servant is called before his master, he does not come with an expectation to hear himself rated for some trivial fault, threatened to be stripped, or used with any other unbecoming language, which mean masters often give to worthy servants; but it is often to know what road he took that he came so readily back according to order; whether he passed by such a ground; if the old man who rents it is in good health; or whether he gave Sir Roger's love to him, or the like.

A man who preserves a respect founded on his benevolence to his dependents lives rather like a prince than a master in his family; his orders are received as favors, rather than duties; and the distinction of approaching him is part of the reward for executing what is commanded by him.

There is another circumstance in which my friend excels in his management, which is the manner of rewarding his servants: he has ever been of opinion that giving his cast clothes to be worn by valets has a very ill effect upon little minds, and creates a silly sense of equality between the parties, in persons affected only with outward things. I have heard him often pleasant on this occasion, and describe a young gentleman abusing his man in that coat which a month or two before was the most pleasing distinction he was conscious of in himself. He would turn his discourse still more pleasantly upon the ladies' bounties of this kind; and I have heard him say he knew a fine woman, who distributed rewards and punishments in giving becoming or unbecoming dresses to her maids.

But my good friend is above these little instances of good-will, in bestowing only trifles on his servants; a good servant to him is sure of having it in his choice very soon of being no servant at all. As I before observed, he is so good an husband,[1] and knows so thoroughly that the skill of the purse is the cardinal virtue of this life, — I say, he knows so well that frugality is the support of generosity, that he can often spare a large fine when a tenement falls,[2] and give that settlement to a good servant who has a mind to go into the world, or make a stranger pay the fine to that servant, for his more comfortable maintenance, if he stays in his service.

A man of honor and generosity considers it would be miserable to himself to have no will but that of another, though it were of the best person breathing, and for that reason goes on as fast as he is able to put his servants into independent livelihoods. The greatest part of Sir Roger's estate is tenanted by persons who have served himself or his ancestors. It was to me extremely pleasant to observe the visit-ants from several parts to welcome his arrival into the country; and all the difference that I could take notice of between the late servants who came to see him, and those who stayed in the family, was that these latter were looked upon as finer gentlemen and better courtiers.

1. We still say to husband one's resources, but the noun hus-band supposes a wife.

2. A legal phrase. When a tenant of a knight made over his land or tenement to another he was required to pay the knight a fine of money.

This manumission and placing them in a way of livelihood I look upon as only what is due to a good servant, which encouragement will make his successor be as diligent, as humble, and as ready as he was. There is something wonderful in the narrowness of those minds which can be pleased and be barren of bounty to those who please them.

One might, on this occasion, recount the sense that great persons in all ages have had of the merit of their dependents, and the heroic services which men have done their masters in the extremity of their fortunes; and shown to their undone patrons that fortune was all the difference between them; but as I design this my speculation only as a gentle admonition to thankless masters, I shall not go out of the occurrences of common life, but assert it as a general observation, that I never saw, but in Sir Roger's family, and one or two more, good servants treated as they ought to be. Sir Roger's kindness extends to their children's children, and this very morning he sent his coachman's grandson to prentice. I shall conclude this paper with an account of a picture in his gallery, where there are many which will deserve my future observation.

At the very upper end of this handsome structure I saw the portraiture of two young men standing in a river, the one naked, the other in a livery. The person supported seemed half dead, but still so much alive as to show in his face exquisite joy and love towards the other. I thought the fainting figure resembled my friend Sir Roger; and looking at the butler, who stood by me, for an account of it, he in-formed me that the person in the livery was a servant of Sir Roger's, who stood on the shore while his master was swimming, and observing him taken with some sudden illness, and sink under water, jumped in and saved him. He told me Sir Roger took off the dress [1] he was in as soon as he came home, and by a great bounty at that time, followed by his favor ever since, had made him master of that pretty seat which we saw at a distance as we came to this house. I remembered indeed Sir Roger said there lived a very worthy gentleman, to whom he was highly obliged, without mentioning anything further. Upon my looking a little dissatisfied at some part of the picture, my attendant informed me that it was against Sir Roger's will, and at the earnest request of the gentleman himself, that he was drawn in the habit in which he had saved his master.

VIII. WILL WIMBLE.

Gratis anhelans, multa agendo nihil agens.[2]
Phædrus, lib. II. fab. v. 3.

As I was yesterday morning walking with Sir Roger before his house, a country fellow brought him a huge fish, which, he told him, Mr. William Wimble had caught that very morning; and that he presented it, with his service to him, and intended to come and dine with him. At the same time he delivered a letter, which my friend read to me as soon as the messenger left him.

"Sir Roger, — I desire you to accept of a jack, which is the best I have caught this season. I intend

---

1. That is, the livery which was a badge of service.
2. Out of breath for nothing, hard at work doing nothing.

to come and stay with you a week, and see how the perch bite in the Black River. I observed with some concern, the last time I saw you upon the bowling-green, that your whip wanted a lash to it; I will bring half a dozen with me that I twisted last week, which I hope will serve you all the time you are in the country. I have not been out of the saddle for six days last past, having been at Eton with Sir John's eldest son. He takes to his learning hugely.

" I am, sir, your humble servant,
"WILL WIMBLE."

This extraordinary letter, and message that accompanied it, made me very curious to know the character and quality of the gentleman who sent them, which I found to be as follows. Will Wimble is younger brother to a baronet, and descended of the ancient family of the Wimbles.[1] He is now between forty and fifty; but being bred to no business and born to no estate, he generally lives with his elder brother as superintendent of his game. He hunts a pack of dogs better than any man in the country, and is very famous for finding out a hare. He is extremely well versed in all the little handicrafts of an

---

1. In *The Tatler*, No. 256, Steele had already drawn almost the same portrait in his character of Mr. Thomas Gules of Gule Hall. "He was the cadet of a very ancient family ; and according to the principles of all the younger brothers of the said family, he had never sullied himself with business ; but had chosen rather to starve like a man of honor, than do anything beneath his quality. He produced several witnesses that he had never employed himself beyond the twisting of a whip, or the making of a pair of nut-crackers, in which he only worked for his diversion, in order to make a present now and then to his friends."

idle man: he makes a may-fly to a miracle, and furnishes the whole country with angle-rods. As he is a good-natured officious fellow, and very much esteemed upon account of his family, he is a welcome guest at every house, and keeps up a good correspondence among all the gentlemen about him. He carries a tulip-root in his pocket from one to another, or exchanges a puppy between a couple of friends that live perhaps in the opposite sides of the county. Will is a particular favorite of all the young heirs, whom he frequently obliges with a net that he has weaved, or a setting-dog that he has made [1] himself. He now and then presents a pair of garters of his own knitting to their mothers or sisters; and raises a great deal of mirth among them, by inquiring as often as he meets them how they wear. These gentleman-like manufactures and obliging little humors make Will the darling of the country.

Sir Roger was proceeding in the character of him, when we saw him make up to us with two or three hazel-twigs in his hand, that he had cut in Sir Roger's woods, as he came through them, in his way to the house. I was very much pleased to observe on one side the hearty and sincere welcome with which Sir Roger received him, and, on the other, the secret joy which his guest discovered at sight of the good old Knight. After the first salutes were over, Will desired Sir Roger to lend him one of his servants to carry a set of shuttlecocks he had with him in a little box to a lady that lived about a mile off, to whom it seems he had promised such a present for above this half year. Sir Roger's back was no sooner turned but honest Will began to tell me of a large cock-

1. That is, trained a setter.

pheasant that he had sprung in one of the neighboring woods, with two or three other adventures of the
same nature. Odd and uncommon characters are the
game that I look for and most delight in; for which
reason I was as much pleased with the novelty of the
person that talked to me, as he could be for his life
with the springing of a pheasant, and therefore listened to him with more than ordinary attention.

In the midst of his discourse the bell rung to dinner, where the gentleman I have been speaking of
had the pleasure of seeing the huge jack he had caught
served up for the first dish in a most sumptuous
manner. Upon our sitting down to it he gave us a
long account how he had hooked it, played with it,
foiled it, and at length drew it out upon the bank,
with several other particulars that lasted all the first
course. A dish of wild fowl that came afterwards
furnished conversation for the rest of the dinner,
which concluded with a late invention of Will's for
improving the quail-pipe.

Upon withdrawing into my room after dinner, I
was secretly touched with compassion towards the
honest gentleman that had dined with us, and could
not but consider, with a great deal of concern, how
so good an heart and such busy hands were wholly
employed in trifles; that so much humanity should be
so little beneficial to others, and so much industry so
little advantageous to himself. The same temper of
mind and application to affairs might have recommended him to the public esteem, and have raised
his fortune in another station of life. What good to
his country or himself might not a trader or merchant have done with such useful though ordinary
qualifications?

Will Wimble's is the case of many a younger brother of a great family, who had rather see their children starve like gentlemen than thrive in a trade or profession that is beneath their quality. This humor fills several parts of Europe with pride and beggary. It is the happiness of a trading nation, like ours, that the younger sons, though uncapable of any liberal art or profession, may be placed in such a way of life as may perhaps enable them to vie with the best of their family. Accordingly, we find several citizens that were launched into the world with narrow fortunes, rising by an honest industry to greater estates than those of their elder brothers. It is not improbable but Will was formerly tried at divinity, law, or physic; and that finding his genius did not lie that way, his parents gave him up at length to his own inventions. But certainly, however improper he might have been for studies of a higher nature, he was perfectly well turned for the occupations of trade and commerce. As I think this is a point which cannot be too much inculcated, I shall desire my reader to compare what I have here written with what I have said in my twenty-first speculation.[1]

1. In the twenty-first paper, or speculation, of *The Spectator*, Addison discusses the overstocking of the three great professions of divinity, law, and physic.

IX. THE COVERLEY LINEAGE.

Abnormis sapiens.[1]

HORACE, *Satires*, II. ii. 3.

I WAS this morning walking in the gallery, when Sir Roger entered at the end opposite to me, and, advancing towards me, said he was glad to meet me among his relations the De Coverleys, and hoped I liked the conversation of so much good company, who were as silent as myself. I knew he alluded to the pictures; and, as he is a gentleman who does not a little value himself upon his ancient descent, I expected he would give me some account of them. We were now arrived at the upper end of the gallery, when the Knight faced towards one of the pictures, and, as we stood before it, he entered into the matter, after his blunt way of saying things as they occur to his imagination without regular introduction or care to preserve the appearance of chain of thought.

"It is," said he, "worth while to consider the force of dress, and how the persons of one age differ from those of another merely by that only. One may observe, also, that the general fashion of one age has been followed by one particular set of people in another, and by them preserved from one generation to another. Thus the vast jetting coat and small bonnet, which was the habit in Harry the Seventh's time, is kept on in the yeomen of the guard; not without a good and politic view, because they look a foot taller, and a foot and an half broader: besides that the cap leaves the face expanded, and consequently more terrible, and fitter to stand at the entrance of palaces.

1. Wise, with a wisdom all his own.

"This predecessor of ours, you see, is dressed after this manner, and his cheeks would be no larger than mine were he in a hat as I am. He was the last man that won a prize in the Tilt Yard (which is now a common street before Whitehall). You see the broken lance that lies there by his right foot: he shivered that lance of his adversary all to pieces; and, bearing himself, look you, sir, in this manner, at the same time he came within the target of the gentleman who rode against him, and taking him with incredible force before him on the pommel of his saddle, he in that manner rid the tournament over, with an air that showed he did it rather to perform the rule of the lists than expose his enemy: however, it appeared he knew how to make use of a victory, and, with a gentle trot, he marched up to a gallery where their mistress sat (for they were rivals) and let him down with laudable courtesy and pardonable insolence. I don't know but it might be exactly where the coffee-house is now.

"You are to know this my ancestor was not only of a military genius, but fit also for the arts of peace, for he played on the bass-viol as well as any gentlemen at court: you see where his viol hangs by his basket-hilt sword. The action at the Tilt Yard you may be sure won the fair lady, who was a maid of honor, and the greatest beauty of her time; here she stands, the next picture. You see, sir, my great-great-great-grandmother has on the new-fashioned petticoat,[1] except that the modern is gathered at the waist: my grandmother appears as if she stood in a large drum, whereas the ladies now walk as if they

1. The new-fashioned petticoat widened gradually from the waist to the ground.

were in a go-cart. For all this lady was bred at court, she became an excellent country wife, she brought ten children, and, when I show you the library, you shall see, in her own hand (allowing for the difference of the language), the best receipt now in England both for an hasty-pudding and a white-pot.

"If you please to fall back a little, because 't is necessary to look at the three next pictures at one view; these are three sisters. She on the right hand, who is so very beautiful, died a maid; the next to her, still handsomer, had the same fate, against her will; this homely thing in the middle had both their portions added to her own, and was stolen by a neighboring gentleman, a man of stratagem and resolution, for he poisoned three mastiffs to come at her, and knocked down two deer-stealers in carrying her off. Misfortunes happen in all families. The theft of this romp and so much money was no great matter [1] to our estate. But the next heir that possessed it was this soft gentleman, whom you see there: observe the small buttons, the little boots, the laces, the slashes about his clothes, and, above all, the posture he is drawn in (which to be sure was his own choosing); you see he sits with one hand on a desk writing and looking as it were another way, like an easy writer, or a sonneteer. He was one of those that had too much wit to know how to live in the world: he was a man of no justice, but great good manners; he ruined everybody that had anything to do with him, but never said a rude thing in his life: the most indolent person in the world, he would sign a deed that passed away half his estate with his

1. That is, was no great gain.

gloves on, but would not put on his hat before a lady if it were to save his country. He is said to be the first that made love by squeezing the hand. He left the estate with ten thousand pounds debt upon it; but, however, by all hands I have been informed that he was every way the finest gentleman in the world. That debt lay heavy on our house for one generation; but it was retrieved by a gift from that honest man you see there, a citizen of our name, but nothing at all akin to us. I know Sir Andrew Freeport has said behind my back that this man was descended from one of the ten children of the maid of honor I showed you above; but it was never made out. We winked at the thing, indeed, because money was wanting at that time."

Here I saw my friend a little embarrassed, and turned my face to the next portraiture.

Sir Roger went on with his account of the gallery in the following manner. "This man" (pointing to him I looked at) "I take to be the honor of our house, Sir Humphrey de Coverley; he was in his dealings as punctual as a tradesman, and as generous as a gentleman. He would have thought himself as much undone by breaking his word, as if it were to be followed by bankruptcy. He served his country as knight of this shire [1] to his dying day. He found it no easy matter to maintain an integrity in his words and actions, even in things that regarded the offices which were incumbent upon him, in the care of his own affairs and relations of life, and therefore dreaded (though he had great talents) to go into employments of state, where he must be exposed to the snares of ambition. Innocence of life and great

1. Member of Parliament for this shire.

ability were the distinguishing parts of his character; the latter, he had often observed, had led to the destruction of the former, and used frequently to lament that great and good had not the same significof cation. He was an excellent husbandman, but had resolved not to exceed such a degree of wealth: all above it he bestowed in secret bounties many years after the sum he aimed at for his own use was attained. Yet he did not slacken his industry, but to a decent old age spent the life and fortune which was superfluous to himself in the service of his friends and neighbors."

Here we were called to dinner, and Sir Roger ended the discourse of this gentleman by telling me, as we followed the servant, that this his ancestor was a brave man, and narrowly escaped being killed in the Civil Wars; "For," said he, "he was sent out of the field upon a private message the day before the battle of Worcester."[1]

The whim of narrowly escaping by having been within a day of danger, with other matters above mentioned, mixed with good sense, left me at a loss whether I was more delighted with my friend's wisdom or simplicity.

X. THE COVERLEY GHOST.

Horror ubique animos, simul ipsa silentia terrent.[2]
VIRGIL, *Æneid*, ii. 755.

AT a little distance from Sir Roger's house, among the ruins of an old abbey, there is a long walk of

1. Fought September 3, 1651.
2. A horror that is all about seizes on the mind ; the very silence is startling.

aged elms, which are shot up so very high, that, when one passes under them, the rooks and crows that rest upon the tops of them seem to be cawing in another region. I am very much delighted with this sort of noise, which I consider as a kind of natural prayer to that Being who supplies the wants of his whole creation, and who, in the beautiful language of the Psalms, feedeth the young ravens that call upon Him.[1] I like this retirement the better, because of an ill report it lies under of being haunted; for which reason (as I have been told in the family) no living creature ever walks in it besides the chaplain. My good friend the butler desired me, with a very grave face, not to venture myself in it after sunset, for that one of the footmen had been almost frighted out of his wits by a spirit that appeared to him in the shape of a black horse without an head; to which he added, that about a month ago one of the maids coming home late that way with a pail of milk upon her head, heard such a rustling among the bushes that she let it fall.

I was taking a walk in this place last night between the hours of nine and ten, and could not but fancy it one of the most proper scenes in the world for a ghost to appear in. The ruins of the abbey are scattered up and down on every side, and half covered with ivy and elder bushes, the harbors of several solitary birds, which seldom make their appearance till the dusk of the evening. The place was formerly a churchyard, and has still several marks in it of graves and burying-places. There is such an echo among the old ruins and vaults, that if you stamp but a little louder than ordinary you hear the

1. The Prayer-book version of Psalm cxlvii. 2.

sound repeated. At the same time the walk of elms, with the croaking of the ravens, which from time to time are heard from the tops of them, looks exceeding solemn and venerable. These objects naturally raise seriousness and attention; and when night heightens the awfulness of the place, and pours out her supernumerary horrors upon everything in it, I do not at all wonder that weak minds fill it with spectres and apparitions.

Mr. Locke, in his chapter of the Association of Ideas, has very curious remarks to show how, by the prejudice of education, one idea often introduces into the mind a whole set that bear no resemblance to one another in the nature of things. Among several examples of this kind, he produces the following instance: — "The ideas of goblins and sprites have really no more to do with darkness than light: yet, let but a foolish maid inculcate these often on the mind of a child, and raise them there together, possibly he shall never be able to separate them again so long as he lives, but darkness shall ever afterwards bring with it those frightful ideas, and they shall be so joined that he can no more bear the one than the other." [1]

As I was walking in this solitude, where the dusk of the evening conspired with so many other occasions of terror, I observed a cow grazing not far from me, which an imagination that was apt to startle might easily have construed into a black horse without an head: and I dare say the poor footman lost his wits upon some such trivial occasion.

My friend Sir Roger has often told me with a great deal of mirth, that at his first coming to his

---

1. *Essay on Human Understanding*, by John Locke, ii. 33, § 10.

estate, he found three parts of his house altogether useless; that the best room in it had the reputation of being haunted, and by that means was locked up; that noises had been heard in his long gallery, so that he could not get a servant to enter it after eight o'clock at night; that the door of one of his chambers was nailed up, because there went a story in the family that a butler had formerly hanged himself in it; and that his mother, who lived to a great age, had shut up half the rooms in the house, in which either her husband, a son, or daughter had died. The Knight seeing his habitation reduced to so small a compass, and himself in a manner shut out of his own house, upon the death of his mother ordered all the apartments to be flung open and exorcised by his chaplain, who lay in every room one after another, and by that means dissipated the fears which had so long reigned in the family.

I should not have been thus particular upon these ridiculous horrors, did I not find them so very much prevail in all parts of the country. At the same time I think a person who is thus terrified with the imagination of ghosts and spectres much more reasonable than one, who, contrary to the reports of all historians, sacred and profane, ancient and modern, and to the traditions of all nations, thinks the appearance of spirits fabulous and groundless: could not I give myself up to this general testimony of mankind, I should to the relations of particular persons who are now living, and whom I cannot distrust in other matters of fact. I might here add, that not only the historians, to whom we may join the poets, but likewise the philosophers of antiquity have favored this opinion. Lucretius himself, though by the course of his philosophy he was obliged to maintain that the soul did not exist separate from the body, makes no doubt of the reality of apparitions, and that men have often appeared after their death. This I think very remarkable: he was so pressed with the matter of fact, which he could not have the confidence to deny, that he was forced to account for it by one of the most absurd unphilosophical notions that was ever started. He tells us that the surfaces of all bodies are perpetually flying off from their respective bodies, one after another; and that these surfaces or thin cases that included each other whilst they were joined in the body, like the coats of an onion, are sometimes seen entire when they are separated from it; by which means we often behold the shapes and shadows of persons who are either dead or absent.[1]

I shall dismiss this paper with a story out of Josephus, not so much for the sake of the story itself as for the moral reflections with which the author concludes it, and which I shall here set down in his own words. "Glaphyra, the daughter of king Archelaus, after the death of her two first husbands (being married to a third, who was brother to her first husband, and so passionately in love with her, that he turned off his former wife to make room for this marriage), had a very odd kind of dream. She fancied that she saw her first husband coming towards her, and that she embraced him with great tenderness; when in the midst of the pleasure which she expressed at the sight of him, he reproached her after the following manner: 'Glaphyra,' says he, 'thou hast made good the old saying, that women are not to be

1. *De Rerum Natura,* iv. 34.

trusted. Was not I the husband of thy virginity? Have I not children by thee? How couldst thou forget our loves so far as to enter into a second marriage, and after that into a third, nay to take for thy husband a man who has so shamelessly crept into the bed of his brother? However, for the sake of our past loves, I shall free thee from thy present reproach, and make thee mine for ever.' Glaphyra told this dream to several women of her acquaintance, and died soon after. I thought this story might not be impertinent in this place, wherein I speak of those kings. Besides that, the example deserves to be taken notice of, as it contains a most certain proof of the immortality of the soul, and of Divine Providence. If any man thinks these facts incredible, let him enjoy his own opinion to himself, but let him not endeavor to disturb the belief of others, who by instances of this nature are excited to the study of virtue." [1]

XI. A SUNDAY AT SIR ROGER'S.

'Αθανάτους μὲν πρῶτα θεούς, νόμῳ ὡς διάκειται,
Τιμᾶ.[2]

PYTHAGORAS.

I AM always very well pleased with a country Sunday, and think, if keeping holy the seventh day were only a human institution, it would be the best method that could have been thought of for the polishing and civilizing of mankind. It is certain the country people would soon degenerate into a kind of savages and

1. Josephus : *The Antiquities of the Jews*, xvii. 15, § 415.
2. First to the immortal gods, as the law directs,
   Give reverence.

barbarians, were there not such frequent returns of a stated time, in which the whole village meet together with their best faces, and in their cleanliest habits, to converse with one another upon indifferent subjects, hear their duties explained to them, and join together in adoration of the Supreme Being. Sunday clears away the rust of the whole week, not only as it refreshes in their minds the notions of religion, but as it puts both the sexes upon appearing in their most agreeable forms, and exerting all such qualities as are apt to give them a figure in the eye of the village. A country fellow distinguishes himself as much in the churchyard, as a citizen does upon the 'Change, the whole parish politics being generally discussed in that place, either after sermon or before the bell rings.

My friend Sir Roger, being a good churchman, has beautified the inside of his church with several texts of his own choosing; he has likewise given a handsome pulpit cloth, and railed in the communion table at his own expense. He has often told me that, at his coming to his estate, he found his parishioners very irregular; and that in order to make them kneel and join in the responses, he gave every one of them a hassock and a Common Prayer Book: and at the same time employed an itinerant singing master, who goes about the country for that purpose, to instruct them rightly in the tunes of the Psalms; upon which they now very much value themselves, and indeed outdo most of the country churches that I have ever heard.

As Sir Roger is landlord to the whole congregation, he keeps them in very good order, and will suffer nobody to sleep in it besides himself; for if by

chance he has been surprised into a short nap at sermon, upon recovering out of it he stands up and
looks about him, and, if he sees anybody else nod-
ding, either wakes them himself, or sends his servant
to them. Several other of the old Knight's particu-
larities break out upon these occasions: sometimes
he will be lengthening out a verse in the singing
Psalms half a minute after the rest of the congregation have done with it ; sometimes, when he is pleased
with the matter of his devotion, he pronounces
"Amen" three or four times to the same prayer;
and sometimes stands up when everybody else is
upon their knees, to count the congregation, or see if
any of his tenants are missing.

I was yesterday very much surprised to hear my
old friend, in the midst of the service, calling out to
one John Matthews to mind what he was about, and
not disturb the congregation. This John Matthews
it seems is remarkable for being an idle fellow, and
at that time was kicking his heels for his diversion.
This authority of the Knight, though exerted in that
odd manner which accompanies him in all circumstances of life, has a very good effect upon the parish, who are not polite enough to see anything ridiculous in his behavior; besides that the general good
sense and worthiness of his character makes his friends
observe these little singularities as foils that rather
set off than blemish his good qualities.

As soon as the sermon is finished, nobody presumes
to stir till Sir Roger is gone out of the church. The
Knight walks down from his seat in the chancel between a double row of his tenants, that stand bowing
to him on each side, and every now and then inquires
how such an one's wife, or mother, or son, or father

do, whom he does not see at church, — which is understood as a secret reprimand to the person that is
absent.

The chaplain has often told me, that upon a cate-
chising day, when Sir Roger has been pleased with a
boy that answers well, he has ordered a Bible to be
given him next day for his encouragement, and sometimes accompanies it with a flitch of bacon to his
mother. Sir Roger has likewise added five pounds a
year to the clerk's place; and that he may encourage
the young fellows to make themselves perfect in the
church service, has promised, upon the death of the
present incumbent, who is very old, to bestow it
according to merit.

The fair understanding between Sir Roger and his
chaplain, and their mutual concurrence in doing
good, is the more remarkable, because the very next
village is famous for the differences and contentions
that rise between the parson and the squire, who live
in a perpetual state of war. The parson is always
preaching at the squire, and the squire, to be re-
venged on the parson, never comes to church. The
squire has made all his tenants atheists and tithe-
stealers; while the parson instructs them every Sunday in the dignity of his order, and insinuates to
them in almost every sermon that he is a better man
than his patron. In short, matters are come to such
an extremity, that the squire has not said his prayers
either in public or private this half year; and that
the parson threatens him, if he does not mend his
manners, to pray for him in the face of the whole
congregation.

Feuds of this nature, though too frequent in the
country, are very fatal to the ordinary people; who

are so used to be dazzled with riches, that they pay
as much deference to the understanding of a man of
an estate as of a man of learning; and are very
hardly brought to regard any truth, how important
soever it may be, that is preached to them, when
they know there are several men of five hundred a
year who do not believe it.

XII. SIR ROGER IN LOVE.

Hærent infixi pectore vultus.[1]
VIRGIL, *Æneid*, iv. 4.

IN my first description of the company in which I
pass most of my time it may be remembered that I
mentioned a great affliction which my friend Sir
Roger had met with in his youth: which was no less
than a disappointment in love. It happened this
evening that we fell into a very pleasing walk at a
distance from his house: as soon as we came into it,
"It is," quoth the good old man, looking round him
with a smile, "very hard, that any part of my land
should be settled upon one who has used me so ill as
the perverse Widow did; and yet I am sure I could
not see a sprig of any bough of this whole walk of
trees, but I should reflect upon her and her severity.
She has certainly the finest hand of any woman in
the world. You are to know this was the place
wherein I used to muse upon her; and by that custom I can never come into it, but the same tender
sentiments revive in my mind as if I had actually
walked with that beautiful creature under these
shades. I have been fool enough to carve her name
on the bark of several of these trees; so unhappy is

1. Her looks abide deep graven in his heart.

the condition of men in love to attempt the removing of their passion by the methods which serve only to imprint it deeper. She has certainly the finest hand of any woman in the world."

Here followed a profound silence; and I was not displeased to observe my friend falling so naturally into a discourse which I had ever before taken notice he industriously avoided. After a very long pause he entered upon an account of this great circumstance in his life, with an air which I thought raised my idea of him above what I had ever had before; and gave me the picture of that cheerful mind of his, before it received that stroke which has ever since affected his words and actions. But he went on as follows: —

"I came to my estate in my twenty-second year, and resolved to follow the steps of the most worthy of my ancestors who have inhabited this spot of earth before me, in all the methods of hospitality and good neighborhood, for the sake of my fame, and in country sports and recreations, for the sake of my health. In my twenty-third year I was obliged to serve as sheriff of the county; and in my servants, officers, and whole equipage, indulged the pleasure of a young man (who did not think ill of his own person) in taking that public occasion of showing my figure[1] and behavior to advantage. You may easily imagine to yourself what appearance I made, who am pretty tall, rid well, and was very well dressed, at the head of a whole county, with music before me, a feather in my hat, and my horse well bitted. I can assure you I was not a little pleased with the kind looks and glances I had from all the balconies and windows as

1. On state occasions the sheriff appeared in court dress.

I rode to the hall where the assizes were held. But
when I came there, a beautiful creature in a widow's
habit sat in court, to hear the event of a cause concerning her dower. This commanding creature (who
was born for destruction of all who behold her) put
on such a resignation in her countenance, and bore
the whispers of all around the court, with such a
pretty uneasiness, I warrant you, and then recovered
herself from one eye to another, till she was perfectly
confused by meeting something so wistful in all she
encountered, that at last, with a murrain to her, she
cast her bewitching eye upon me. I no sooner met
it but I bowed like a great surprised booby; and
knowing her cause to be the first which came on, I
cried, like a captivated calf as I was, 'Make way for
the defendant's witnesses.' This sudden partiality
made all the county immediately see the sheriff also
was become a slave to the fine widow. During the
time her cause was upon trial, she behaved herself, I
warrant you, with such a deep attention to her business, took opportunities to have little billets handed
to her counsel, then would be in such a pretty confusion, occasioned, you must know, by acting before so
much company, that not only I but the whole court
was prejudiced in her favor; and all that the next
heir to her husband had to urge was thought so
groundless and frivolous, that when it came to her
counsel to reply, there was not half so much said as
every one besides in the court thought he could have
urged to her advantage. You must understand, sir,
this perverse woman is one of those unaccountable
creatures, that secretly rejoice in the admiration of
men, but indulge themselves in no further consequences. Hence it is that she has ever had a train

of admirers, and she removes from her slaves in town
to those in the country, according to the seasons of
the year. She is a reading lady, and far gone in the
pleasures of friendship: she is always accompanied
by a confidante, who is witness to her daily protesta-
tions against our sex, and consequently a bar to her
first steps towards love, upon the strength of her own
maxims and declarations.

"However, I must needs say this accomplished
mistress of mine has distinguished me above the rest,
and has been known to declare Sir Roger de Coverley was the tamest and most human of all the brutes
in the country. I was told she said so by one who
thought he rallied me; but upon the strength of this
slender encouragement of being thought least detesta-
ble, I made new liveries, new-paired my coach-horses,
sent them all to town to be bitted, and taught to
throw their legs well, and move all together, before I
pretended to cross the country and wait upon her.
As soon as I thought my retinue suitable to the character of my fortune and youth, I set out from hence
to make my addresses. The particular skill of this
lady has ever been to inflame your wishes, and yet
command respect. To make her mistress of this art,
she has a greater share of knowledge, wit, and good
sense than is usual even among men of merit. Then
she is beautiful beyond the race of women. If you
won't let her go on with a certain artifice with her
eyes, and the skill of beauty, she will arm herself
with her real charms, and strike you with admiration. It is certain that if you were to behold the
whole woman, there is that dignity in her aspect,
that composure in her motion, that complacency in
her manner, that if her form makes you hope, her

merit makes you fear. But then again, she is such
a desperate scholar, that no country gentleman can
approach her without being a jest. As I was going
to tell you, when I came to her house I was admitted
to her presence with great civility; at the same time
she placed herself to be first seen by me in such an
attitude, as I think you call the posture of a picture,
that she discovered new charms, and I at last came
towards her with such an awe as made me speechless.
This she no sooner observed but she made her advantage of it, and began a discourse to me concerning
love and honor, as they both are followed by pretenders, and the real votaries to them. When she had
discussed these points in a discourse, which I verily
believe was as learned as the best philosopher in
Europe could possibly make, she asked me whether
she was so happy as to fall in with my sentiments on
these important particulars. Her confidante sat by
her, and upon my being in the last confusion and
silence, this malicious aid of hers turning to her
says, 'I am very glad to observe Sir Roger pauses
upon this subject, and seems resolved to deliver all
his sentiments upon the matter when he pleases to
speak.' They both kept their countenances, and after
I had sat half an hour meditating how to behave
before such profound casuists, I rose up and took my
leave. Chance has since that time thrown me very
often in her way, and she as often has directed a discourse to me which I do not understand. This bar-
barity has kept me ever at a distance from the most
beautiful object my eyes ever beheld. It is thus
also she deals with all mankind, and you must make
love to her, as you would conquer the sphinx, by
posing her. But were she like other women, and

that there were any talking to her, how constant must
the pleasure of that man be, who could converse with
a creature — But, after all, you may be sure her
heart is fixed on some one or other; and yet I have
been credibly informed — but who can believe half
that is said? After she had done speaking to me,
she put her hand to her bosom and adjusted her
tucker. Then she cast her eyes a little down, upon
my beholding her too earnestly. They say she sings
excellently: her voice in her ordinary speech has
something in it inexpressibly sweet. You must know
I dined with her at a public table the day after I
first saw her, and she helped me to some tansy [1] in the
eye of all the gentlemen in the country: she has
certainly the finest hand of any woman in the world.
I can assure you, sir, were you to behold her, you
would be in the same condition; for as her speech is
music, her form is angelic. But I find I grow irregular while I am talking of her; but indeed it would
be stupidity to be unconcerned at such perfection.
Oh the excellent creature! she is as inimitable to all
women as she is inaccessible to all men."

I found my friend begin to rave, and insensibly
led him towards the house, that we might be joined
by some other company; and am convinced that the

1. A favorite dish of the seventeenth century. The following
recipe for preparing it is from *A Closet of Rarities*, 1706.
"Take about a dozen new-laid eggs, beat them up with three
pints of cream, strain them through a coarse linen cloth, and
put in of the strained juices of endive, spinach, sorrel, and
tansy, each three spoonfuls ; half a grated nutmeg, four ounces
of fine sugar, and a little salt and rose-water. Put it with a
slight laying of butter under it into a shallow pewter dish, and
bake it in a moderately heated oven. Scrape over it loaf sugar,
sprinkle rose-water, and serve it up."

Widow is the secret cause of all that inconsistency which appears in some parts of my friend's discourse; though he has so much command of himself as not directly to mention her, yet according to that [passage] of Martial, which one knows not how to render in English, *Dum tacet hanc loquitur.*[1] I shall end this paper with that whole epigram, which represents with much humor my honest friend's condition.

> Quicquid agit Rufus, nihil est, nisi Nævia Rufo,
>   Si gaudet, si flet, si tacet, hanc loquitur:
> Cœnat, propinat, poscit, negat, annuit, una est
>   Nævia; si non sit Nævia, mutus erit.
> Scriberet hesternâ patri cûm luce salutem,
>   Nævia lux, inquit, Nævia lumen, ave.

> Let Rufus weep, rejoice, stand, sit, or walk,
> Still he can nothing but of Nævia talk;
> Let him eat, drink, ask questions, or dispute,
> Still he must speak of Nævia, or be mute;
> He writ to his father, ending with this line,
> "I am, my lovely Nævia, ever thine."

XIII. THE COVERLEY ECONOMY.

Paupertatis pudor et fuga.[2]
HORACE, *Epistles*, I. xviii. 24.

ECONOMY in our affairs has the same effect upon our fortunes which good breeding has upon our conversations. There is a pretending behavior in both cases, which, instead of making men esteemed, renders them both miserable and contemptible. We had yesterday at Sir Roger's a set of country gentlemen who dined with him: and after dinner the glass

1. Book I. Epigram 69. While he is silent he is speaking of her.
2. The shame and dread of poverty.

was taken, by those who pleased, pretty plentifully. Among others I observed a person of a tolerable good aspect, who seemed to be more greedy of liquor than any of the company, and yet, methought, he did not taste it with delight. As he grew warm, he was suspicious of everything that was said; and as he advanced towards being fuddled, his humor grew worse. At the same time his bitterness seemed to be rather an inward dissatisfaction in his own mind than any dislike he had taken at the company. Upon hearing his name, I knew him to be a gentleman of a considerable fortune in this county, but greatly in debt. What gives the unhappy man this peevishness of spirit, is, that his estate is dipped, and is eating out with usury; and yet he has not the heart to sell any part of it. His proud stomach, at the cost of restless nights, constant inquietudes, danger of affronts, and a thousand nameless inconveniences, preserves this canker in his fortune, rather than it shall be said he is a man of fewer hundreds a year than he has been commonly reputed. Thus he endures the torment of poverty, to avoid the name of being less rich. If you go to his house you see great plenty, but served in a manner that shows it is all unnatural, and that the master's mind is not at home. There is a certain waste and carelessness in the air of everything, and the whole appears but a covered indigence, a magnificent poverty. That neatness and cheerfulness which attends the table of him who lives within compass is wanting, and exchanged for a libertine way of service in all about him.

This gentleman's conduct, though a very common way of management, is as ridiculous as that officer's would be, who had but few men under his command, and should take the charge of an extent of country rather than of a small pass. To pay for, personate, and keep in a man's hands a greater estate than he really has, is of all others the most unpardonable vanity, and must in the end reduce the man who is guilty of it to dishonor. Yet if we look round us in any county of Great Britain, we shall see many in this fatal error; if that may be called by so soft a name which proceeds from a false shame of appearing what they really are, when the contrary behavior would in a short time advance them to the condition which they pretend to.

Laertes has fifteen hundred pounds a year, which is mortgaged for six thousand pounds; but it is impossible to convince him that if he sold as much as would pay off that debt he would save four shillings in the pound,[1] which he gives for the vanity of being the reputed master of it. Yet if Laertes did this, he would perhaps be easier in his own fortune; but then Irus, a fellow of yesterday, who has but twelve hundred a year, would be his equal. Rather than this shall be, Laertes goes on to bring well-born beggars into the world, and every twelve month charges his estate with at least one year's rent more by the birth of a child.

Laertes and Irus are neighbors, whose ways of living are an abomination to each other. Irus is moved by the fear of poverty, and Laertes by the shame of it. Though the motive of action is of so near affinity in both, and may be resolved into this, "That to each of them poverty is the greatest of all evils," yet are their manners very widely differ-

1. The rate of the land tax.

ent.   Shame of poverty makes Laertes launch into
unnecessary equipage, vain expense, and lavish entertainments; fear of poverty makes Irus allow himself only plain necessaries, appear without a servant,
sell his own corn, attend his laborers, and be himself
a laborer.   Shame of poverty makes Laertes go
every day a step nearer to it, and fear of poverty
stirs up Irus to make every day some further progress from it.

These different motives produce the excesses which
men are guilty of in the negligence of and pro-
vision for themselves.   Usury, stock-jobbing, extor-
tion, and oppression have their seed in the dread of
want; and vanity, riot, and prodigality, from the
shame of it: but both these excesses are infinitely
below the pursuit of a reasonable creature.   After
we have taken care to command so much as is necessary for maintaining ourselves in the order of men
suitable to our character, the care of superfluities is
a vice no less extravagant than the neglect of necessaries would have been before.

Certain it is, that they are both out of nature,
when she is followed with reason and good sense.   It
is from this reflection that I always read Mr. Cowley
with the greatest pleasure.   His magnanimity is as
much above that of other considerable men as his
understanding; and it is a true distinguishing spirit
in the elegant author[1] who published his works, to
dwell so much upon the temper of his mind and the
moderation of his desires.   By this means he has ren-
dered his friend as amiable as famous.   That state of
life which bears the face of poverty with Mr. Cow-

1. Dr. Thomas Sprat, the Bishop of Rochester, who introduced
Cowley's works with a Life.

ley's *great Vulgar* [1] is admirably described; and it is no small satisfaction to those of the same turn of desire, that he produces the authority of the wisest men of the best age of the world to strengthen his opinion of the ordinary pursuits of mankind.

It would methinks be no ill maxim of life, if according to that ancestor of Sir Roger whom I lately mentioned, every man would point to himself what sum he would resolve not to exceed. He might by this means cheat himself into a tranquillity on this side of that expectation, or convert what he should get above it to nobler uses than his own pleasures or necessities. This temper of mind would exempt a man from an ignorant envy of restless men above him, and a more inexcusable contempt of happy men below him. This would be sailing by some compass, living with some design; but to be eternally bewildered in prospects of future gain, and putting on unnecessary armor against improbable blows of fortune, is a mechanic being which has not good sense for its direction, but is carried on by a sort of acquired instinct towards things below our consideration, and unworthy our esteem.

It is possible that the tranquillity I now enjoy at Sir Roger's may have created in me this way of thinking, which is so abstracted from the common relish of the world: but as I am now in a pleasing arbor, surrounded with a beautiful landscape, I find no inclination so strong as to continue in these mansions, so remote from the ostentatious scenes of life;

1. See Cowley's Paraphrase of Horace's ode, *Odi Profanum Vulgus:* —

> "Hence, ye profane, I hate ye all,
> Both the great vulgar and the small."

and am at this present writing philosopher enough to conclude with Mr. Cowley,

> If e'er ambition did my fancy cheat,
> With any wish so mean as to be great,
> Continue, Heaven, still from me to remove
> The humble blessings of that life I love! [1]

XIV. BODILY EXERCISE.

Ut sit mens sana in corpore sano.[2]
JUVENAL, *Satire* x. 356.

BODILY labor is of two kinds, either that which a man submits to for his livelihood, or that which he undergoes for his pleasure. The latter of them generally changes the name of labor for that of exercise, but differs only from ordinary labor as it rises from another motive.

A country life abounds in both these kinds of labor, and for that reason gives a man a greater stock of health, and consequently a more perfect enjoyment of himself, than any other way of life. I consider the body as a system of tubes and glands, or, to use a more rustic phrase, a bundle of pipes and strainers, fitted to one another after so wonderful a manner as to make a proper engine for the soul to work with. This description does not only comprehend the bowels, bones, tendons, veins, nerves, and arteries, but every muscle and every ligature, which is a composition of fibres, that are so many imperceptible tubes or pipes interwoven on all sides with invisible glands or strainers.

This general idea of a human body, without con-

1. From Cowley's Essay *Of Greatness.*
2. Pray for a sound mind in a sound body.

sidering it in its niceties of anatomy, lets us see how absolutely necessary labor is for the right preservation of it. There must be frequent motions and agitations, to mix, digest, and separate the juices contained in it, as well as to clear and cleanse that infinitude of pipes and strainers, of which it is composed, and to give their solid parts a more firm and lasting tone. Labor or exercise ferments the humors, casts them into their proper channels, throws off redundancies, and helps nature in those secret distributions, without which the body cannot subsist in its vigor, nor the soul act with cheerfulness.

I might here mention the effects which this has upon all the faculties of the mind, by keeping the understanding clear, the imagination untroubled, and refining those spirits that are necessary for the proper exertion of our intellectual faculties, during the present laws of union between soul and body. It is to a neglect in this particular that we must ascribe the spleen which is so frequent in men of studious and sedentary tempers, as well as the vapors to which those of the other sex are so often subject.

Had not exercise been absolutely necessary for our well-being, nature would not have made the body so proper for it, by giving such an activity to the limbs, and such a pliancy to every part as necessarily produce those compressions, extensions, contortions, dilatations, and all other kinds of motions that are necessary for the preservation of such a system of tubes and glands as has been before mentioned. And that we might not want inducements to engage us in such an exercise of the body as is proper for its welfare, it is so ordered that nothing valuable can be procured without it. Not to mention riches and honor, even

food and raiment are not to be come at without the
toil of the hands and sweat of the brows. Providence
furnishes materials but expects that we should work
them up ourselves. The earth must be labored[1] before it gives its increase, and when it is forced into
its several products, how many hands must they pass
through before they are fit for use! Manufactures,
trade, and agriculture naturally employ more than
nineteen parts of the species in twenty: and as for
those who are not obliged to labor, by the condition
in which they are born, they are more miserable than
the rest of mankind unless they indulge themselves in
that voluntary labor which goes by the name of exercise.

My friend Sir Roger has been an indefatigable
man in business of this kind, and has hung several
parts of his house with the trophies of his former
labors. The walls of his great hall are covered with
the horns of several kinds of deer that he has killed
in the chase, which he thinks the most valuable furniture of his house, as they afford him frequent topics
of discourse, and show that he has not been idle.
At the lower end of the hall is a large otter's skin
stuffed with hay, which his mother ordered to be
hung up in that manner, and the Knight looks upon
with great satisfaction, because it seems he was but
nine years old when his dog killed him. A little
room adjoining to the hall is a kind of arsenal filled
with guns of several sizes and inventions, with which
the Knight has made great havoc in the woods, and
destroyed many thousands of pheasants, partridges,
and woodcocks. ' His stable doors are patched with
noses that belonged to foxes of the Knight's own

---

1. Observe the analogous use of " laborer."

hunting down. Sir Roger showed me one of them that for distinction's sake has a brass nail struck through it, which cost him about fifteen hours' riding, carried him through half a dozen counties, killed him a brace of geldings, and lost above half his dogs. This the Knight looks upon as one of the greatest exploits of his life. The perverse Widow, whom I have given some account of, was the death of several foxes; for Sir Roger has told me that in the course of his amours he patched the western door of his stable. Whenever the Widow was cruel, the foxes were sure to pay for it. In proportion as his passion for the Widow abated and old age came on, he left off foxhunting; but a hare is not yet safe that sits within ten miles of his house.

There is no kind of exercise which I would so recommend to my readers of both sexes as this of riding, as there is none which so much conduces to health, and is every way accommodated to the body, according to the idea which I have given of it. Doctor Sydenham is very lavish in its praises; and if the English reader will see the mechanical effects of it described at length, he may find them in a book published not many years since under the title of *Medicina Gymnastica.*[1] For my own part, when I am in town, for want of these opportunities, I exercise myself an hour every morning upon a dumb-bell that is placed in a corner of my room, and pleases me the more because it does every thing I require of it in the most profound silence. My landlady and her daughters are so well acquainted with my hours of exercise, that they never come into my room to disturb me whilst I am ringing.

1. *Medicina Gymnastica ; or a Treatise concerning the Power of Exercise.* By Francis Fuller, M. A.

When I was some years younger than I am at present, I used to employ myself in a more laborious diversion, which I learned from a Latin treatise of exercises[1] that is written with great erudition; it is there called the σκιομαχία, or the fighting with a man's own shadow, and consists in the brandishing of two short sticks grasped in each hand, and loaden with plugs of lead at either end. This opens the chest, exercises the limbs, and gives a man all the pleasure of boxing, without the blows. I could wish that several learned men would lay out that time which they employ in controversies and disputes about nothing, in this method of fighting with their own shadows. It might conduce very much to evaporate the spleen, which makes them uneasy to the public as well as to themselves.

To conclude: As I am a compound of soul and body, I consider myself as obliged to a double scheme of duties; and I think I have not fulfilled the business of the day when I do not thus employ the one in labor and exercise, as well as the other in study and contemplation.

XV. THE COVERLEY HUNT.

Vocat ingenti clamore Cithœron,
Taygetique canes.[2]

VIRGIL, *Georgics*, iii. 43.

THOSE who have searched into human nature observe, that nothing so much shows the nobleness of the soul, as that its felicity consists in action.

---

1. *Artis Gymnasticœ apud antiquos.* Venice, 1509.
2.   Cithæron calls aloud with boisterous voice,
       And the hounds of Taygetus bay.

Every man has such an active principle in him, that he will find out something to employ himself upon, in whatever place or state of life he is posted. I have heard of a gentleman who was under close confinement in the Bastile seven years; during which time he amused himself in scattering a few small pins about his chamber, gathering them up again, and placing them in different figures on the arm of a great chair. He often told his friends afterwards, that unless he had found out this piece of exercise, he verily believed he should have lost his senses.

After what has been said, I need not inform my readers, that Sir Roger, with whose character I hope they are at present pretty well acquainted,[1] has in his youth gone through the whole course of those rural diversions which the country abounds in; and which seem to be extremely well suited to that laborious industry a man may observe here in a far greater degree than in towns and cities. I have before hinted at some of my friend's exploits: he has in his youthful days taken forty coveys of partridges in a season; and tired many a salmon with a line consisting but of a single hair. The constant thanks and good wishes of the neighborhood always attended him on account of his remarkable enmity towards foxes; having destroyed more of those vermin in one year than it was thought the whole country could have produced. Indeed, the Knight does not scruple to own among his most intimate friends, that in order to establish his reputation this way, he has secretly sent for great numbers of them out of other

1. This reads like the sentence of a fresh contributor to the series. One would scarcely expect Addison or Steele, who had been closely occupied with the theme, to interject the phrase.

counties, which he used to turn loose about the country by night, that he might the better signalize himself in their destruction the next day. His hunting
horses were the finest and best managed in all these
parts: his tenants are still full of the praises of a
gray stone horse that unhappily staked himself several years since, and was buried with great solemnity
in the orchard.

Sir Roger, being at present too old for foxhunting, to keep himself in action, has disposed of his
beagles and got a pack of stop-hounds. What these
want in speed he endeavors to make amends for by
the deepness of their mouths and the variety of their
notes, which are suited in such manner to each other
that the whole cry makes up a complete concert.[1]
He is so nice in this particular, that a gentleman
having made him a present of a very fine hound the
other day, the Knight returned it by the servant with
a great many expressions of civility; but desired him
to tell his master that the dog he had sent was indeed
a most excellent bass, but that at present he only
wanted a counter-tenor. Could I believe my friend

1. "As to dogs, the difference is great between a hunt now and
a hunt in *The Spectator's* time. Since the early years of the last
century, the modern foxhound has come into existence, while the
beagle and the deep-flewed southern hare-hound, nearly resembling the bloodhound, with its sonorous note, has become almost
extinct. Absolutely extinct also is the old care to attune the
voices of the pack. Henry II., in his breeding of hounds, is said
to have been careful not only that they should be fleet, but also
'well-tongued and consonous;' the same care in Elizabeth's
time is, in the passage quoted by *The Spectator*, attributed by
Shakespeare to Duke Theseus; and the paper itself shows that
care was taken to match the voices of a pack in the reign also
of Queen Anne. This has now been for some time absolutely
disregarded." — Note in Morley's edition of *The Spectator*.

had ever read Shakespeare I should certainly conclude he had taken the hint from Theseus in the
Midsummer Night's Dream: —

> My hounds are bred out of the Spartan kind,
> So flew'd, so sanded ; and their heads are hung
> With ears that sweep away the morning dew ;
> Crook-knee'd and dew-lapp'd like Thessalian bulls ;
> Slow in pursuit, but match'd in mouth like bells,
> Each under each : a cry more tuneable
> Was never holla'd to, nor cheer'd with horn.

Sir Roger is so keen at this sport that he has been
out almost every day since I came down; and upon
the chaplain's offering to lend me his easy pad, I was
prevailed on yesterday morning to make one of the
company. I was extremely pleased, as we rid along,
to observe the general benevolence of all the neighborhood towards my friend. The farmers' sons
thought themselves happy if they could open a gate
for the good old Knight as he passed by; which he
generally requited with a nod or a smile, and a kind
inquiry after their fathers and uncles.

After we had rid about a mile from home, we
came upon a large heath, and the sportsmen began
to beat. They had done so for some time, when, as
I was at a little distance from the rest of the company, I saw a hare pop out from a small furze-brake
almost under my horse's feet. I marked the way she
took, which I endeavored to make the company sensible of by extending my arm; but to no purpose, till
Sir Roger, who knows that none of my extraordinary
motions are insignificant, rode up to me, and asked
me if puss was gone that way. Upon my answering "Yes," he immediately called in the dogs and
put them upon the scent. As they were going off,
I heard one of the country-fellows muttering to his

companion that 't was a wonder they had not lost all
their sport, for want of the silent gentleman's crying
"Stole away!"

This, with my aversion to leaping hedges, made
me withdraw to a rising ground, from whence I could
have the picture of the whole chase, without the
fatigue of keeping in with the hounds. The hare
immediately threw them above a mile behind her;
but I was pleased to find that instead of running
straight forwards, or in hunter's language, "Flying
the country," as I was afraid she might have done,
she wheeled about, and described a sort of circle
round the hill where I had taken my station, in such
manner as gave me a very distinct view of the
sport. I could see her first pass by, and the dogs
some time afterwards unravelling the whole track she
had made, and following her through all her doubles.
I was at the same time delighted in observing that
deference which the rest of the pack paid to each
particular hound, according to the character he had
acquired amongst them: if they were at fault, and
an old hound of reputation opened but once, he was
immediately followed by the whole cry; while a raw
dog, or one who was a noted liar, might have yelped
his heart out, without being taken notice of.

The hare now, after having squatted two or three
times, and been put up again as often, came still
nearer to the place where she was at first started.
The dogs pursued her, and these were followed by
the jolly Knight, who rode upon a white gelding,
encompassed by his tenants and servants, and cheer-
ing his hounds with all the gaiety of five-and-twenty.
One of the sportsmen rode up to me, and told me
that he was sure the chase was almost at an end,

because the old dogs, which had hitherto lain behind,
now headed the pack. The fellow was in the right.
Our hare took a large field just under us, followed by
the full cry "In view." I must confess the bright-
ness of the weather, the cheerfulness of everything
around me, the chiding of the hounds, which was
returned upon us in a double echo from two neighboring hills, with the holloaing of the sportsmen,
and the sounding of the horn, lifted my spirits into
a most lively pleasure, which I freely indulged
because I was sure it was innocent. If I was under
any concern, it was on the account of the poor hare,
that was now quite spent, and almost within the
reach of her enemies; when the huntsman, getting
forward, threw down his pole before the dogs. They
were now within eight yards of that game which they
had been pursuing for almost as many hours; yet on
the signal before-mentioned they all made a sudden
stand, and though they continued opening as much
as before, durst not once attempt to pass beyond the
pole. At the same time Sir Roger rode forward,
and alighting, took up the hare in his arms; which
he soon delivered up to one of his servants with an
order, if she could be kept alive, to let her go in his
great orchard; where it seems he has several of these
prisoners of war, who live together in a very comfortable captivity. I was highly pleased to see the
discipline of the pack, and the good-nature of the
Knight, who could not find in his heart to murder a
creature that had given him so much diversion.

As we were returning home, I remembered that
Monsieur Pascal, in his most excellent discourse on
the Misery of Man, tells us, that all our endeavors
after greatness proceed from nothing but a desire of

being surrounded by a multitude of persons and affairs that may hinder us from looking into ourselves, which is a view we cannot bear. He afterwards goes on to show that our love of sports comes from the same reason, and is particularly severe upon hunting. "What," says he, "unless it be to drown thought, can make men throw away so much time and pains upon a silly animal, which they might buy cheaper in the market?" The foregoing reflection is certainly just, when a man suffers his whole mind to be drawn into his sports, and altogether loses himself in the woods; but does not affect those who propose a far more laudable end from this exercise, I mean the preservation of health, and keeping all the organs of the soul in a condition to execute her orders. Had that incomparable person, whom I last quoted, been a little more indulgent to himself in this point, the world might probably have enjoyed him much longer; whereas through too great an application to his studies in his youth, he contracted that ill habit of body, which, after a tedious sickness, carried him off in the fortieth year of his age; and the whole history we have of his life till that time is but one continued account of the behavior of a noble soul struggling under innumerable pains and distempers.

For my own part I intend to hunt twice a week during my stay with Sir Roger; and shall prescribe the moderate use of this exercise to all my country friends, as the best kind of physic for mending a bad constitution, and preserving a good one.[1]

1. It is not impossible that as Addison appears to have had a genuine aversion to field sports, this subject was turned over to a writer who was familiar with hunting, since the portrait of a country gentleman like Sir Roger would be imperfect without this feature. Budgell has preserved well the Spectator's character.

I cannot do this better, than in the following lines out of Mr. Dryden: —

> The first physicians by debauch were made;
> Excess began, and sloth sustains the trade.
> By chase our long-lived fathers earned their food;
> Toil strung the nerves, and purified the blood;
> But we their sons, a pamper'd race of men,
> Are dwindled down to threescore years and ten.
> Better to hunt in fields for health unbought
> Than fee the doctor for a nauseous draught.
> The wise for cure on exercise depend:
> God never made His work for man to mend.[1]

XVI. THE COVERLEY WITCH.

Ipsi sibi somnia fingunt.[2]
VIRGIL, *Eclogues*, viii. 108.

THERE are some opinions in which a man should stand neuter, without engaging his assent to one side or the other. Such a hovering faith as this, which refuses to settle upon any determination, is absolutely necessary to a mind that is careful to avoid errors and prepossessions. When the arguments press equally on both sides in matters that are indifferent to us, the safest method is to give up ourselves to neither.

It is with this temper of mind that I consider the subject of witchcraft. When I hear the relations that are made from all parts of the world, not only from Norway and Lapland, from the East and West Indies, but from every particular nation in Europe, I cannot forbear thinking that there is such an intercourse and commerce with evil spirits as that which we express by the name of witchcraft. But when I

1. *An Epistle to his kinsman, J. Dryden, Esq., of Chesterton.*
2. They feign their own dreams.

consider that the ignorant and credulous parts of the world abound most in these relations, and that the persons among us who are supposed to engage in such an infernal commerce are people of a weak understanding and a crazed imagination, and at the same time reflect upon the many impostures and delusions of this nature that have been detected in all ages, I endeavor to suspend my belief till I hear more certain accounts than any which have yet come to my knowledge. In short, when I consider the question, whether there are such persons in the world as those we call witches, my mind is divided between the two opposite opinions: or rather (to speak my thoughts freely) I believe in general that there is, and has been, such a thing as witchcraft ; but at the same time can give no credit to any particular instance of it.

I am engaged in this speculation by some occurrences that I met with yesterday, which I shall give my reader an account of at large. As I was walking with my friend Sir Roger by the side of one of his woods, an old woman applied herself to me for my charity. Her dress and figure put me in mind of the following description in Otway : —

> In a close lane as I pursued my journey,
> I spied a wrinkled hag, with age grown double,
> Picking dry sticks, and mumbling to herself.
> Her eyes with scalding rheum were gall'd and red ;
> Cold palsy shook her head ; her hands seem'd wither'd ;
> And on her crooked shoulders had she wrapp'd
> The tatter'd remnants of an old striped hanging,
> Which served to keep her carcase from the cold :
> So there was nothing of a piece about her.
> Her lower weeds were all o'er coarsely patch'd
> With diff'rent color'd rags, black, red, white, yellow,
> And seem'd to speak variety of wretchedness.[1]

1. *The Orphan*, act ii.

As I was musing on this description, and comparing it with the object before me, the Knight told me that this very old woman had the reputation of a witch all over the country, that her lips were observed to be always in motion, and that there was not a switch about her house which her neighbors did not believe had carried her several hundreds of miles. If she chanced to stumble, they always found sticks or straws that lay in the figure of a cross before her. If she made any mistake at church, and cried *Amen* in a wrong place, they never failed to conclude that she was saying her prayers backwards. There was not a maid in the parish that would take a pin of her, though she would offer a bag of money with it. She goes by the name of Moll White, and has made the country ring with several imaginary exploits which are palmed upon her. If the dairy maid does not make her butter come so soon as she should have it, Moll White is at the bottom of the churn. If a horse sweats in the stable, Moll White has been upon his back. If a hare makes an unexpected escape from the hounds, the huntsman curses Moll White. "Nay," says Sir Roger, "I have known the master of the pack, upon such an occasion, send one of his servants to see if Moll White had been out that morning."

This account raised my curiosity so far, that I begged my friend Sir Roger to go with me into her hovel, which stood in a solitary corner under the side of the wood. Upon our first entering Sir Roger winked to me, and pointed at something that stood behind the door, which, upon looking that way, I found to be an old broomstaff. At the same time he whispered me in the ear to take notice of a tabby cat that sat in the chimney corner, which, as the old Knight told me, lay under as bad a report as Moll White herself; for besides that Moll is said often to accompany her in the same shape, the cat is reported to have spoken twice or thrice in her life, and to have played several pranks above the capacity of an ordinary cat.

I was secretly concerned to see human nature in so much wretchedness and disgrace, but at the same time could not forbear smiling to hear Sir Roger, who is a little puzzled about the old woman, advising her as a justice of peace to avoid all communication with the devil, and never to hurt any of her neighbors' cattle. We concluded our visit with a bounty, which was very acceptable.

In our return home, Sir Roger told me that old Moll had been often brought before him for making children spit pins, and giving maids the night-mare ; and that the country people would be tossing her into a pond [1] and trying experiments with her every day, if it was not for him and his chaplain.

I have since found upon inquiry that Sir Roger was several times staggered with the reports that had been brought him concerning this old woman, and would frequently have bound her over to the county sessions had not his chaplain with much ado persuaded him to the contrary.

I have been the more particular in this account, because I hear there is scarce a village in England that has not a Moll White in it. When an old woman begins to dote, and grow chargeable to a par-

---

1. To see if she would float or sink. If she floated she was a witch, so that it was small comfort to the unfortunate person to save herself from drowning.

ish, she is generally turned into a witch, and fills the whole country with extravagant fancies, imaginary distempers and terrifying dreams. In the mean time, the poor wretch that is the innocent occasion of so many evils begins to be frighted at herself, and sometimes confesses secret commerce and familiari-- ties that her imagination forms in a delirious old age. This frequently cuts off charity from the greatest objects of compassion, and inspires people with a malevolence towards those poor decrepit parts of our species, in whom human nature is defaced by infirm- ity and dotage.[1]

XVII. SIR ROGER AND LOVE-MAKING.

Hæret lateri lethalis arundo.[2]
VIRGIL, *Æneid*, iv. 73.

THIS agreeable seat is surrounded with so many pleasing walks which are struck out of a wood in the midst of which the house stands, that one can hardly ever be weary of rambling from one labyrinth of delight to another. To one used to live in a city the charms of the country are so exquisite that the mind is lost in a certain transport which raises us above ordinary life, and is yet not strong enough to be inconsistent with tranquillity. This state of mind was I in, ravished with the murmur of waters, the whisper of breezes, the singing of birds; and whether I looked up to the heavens, down on the earth, or turned to the prospects around me, still struck with

1. The witchcraft delusion in Salem Village, Massachusetts, raged through the spring and summer of 1692. In England, the last condemnation to death for witchcraft was in 1712.

2. The fatal arrow rankles in his side.

new sense of pleasure; when I found by the voice of
my friend, who walked by me, that we had insensibly
strolled into the grove sacred to the Widow. "This
woman," says he, "is of all others the most unintelli-
gible; she either designs to marry, or she does not.
What is the most perplexing of all is, that she doth
not either say to her lovers she has any resolution
against that condition of life in general, or that she
banishes them; but conscious of her own merit, she
permits their addresses without fear of any ill consequence, or want of respect, from their rage or de-
spair. She has that in her aspect against which it
is impossible to offend. A man whose thoughts are
constantly bent upon so agreeable an object must be
excused if the ordinary occurrences in conversation
are below his attention. I call her indeed perverse,
but, alas! why do I call her so? Because her superior merit is such, that I cannot approach her without awe, that my heart is checked by too much
esteem: I am angry that her charms are not more
accessible, that I am more inclined to worship than
salute her: how often have I wished her unhappy
that I might have an opportunity of serving her?
and how often troubled in that very imagination, at
giving her the pain of being obliged? Well, I have
led a miserable life in secret upon her account; but
fancy she would have condescended to have some
regard for me, if it had not been for that watchful
animal her confidante.

"Of all persons under the sun," continued he,
calling me by my name, "be sure to set a mark
upon confidantes; they are of all people the most
impertinent. What is most pleasant to observe in
them is that they assume to themselves the merit of

the persons whom they have in their custody. Ores-
tilla is a great fortune,[1] and in wonderful danger of
surprises, therefore full of suspicions of the least
indifferent thing, particularly careful of new acquaintance, and of growing too familiar with the old.
Themista, her favorite woman, is every whit as careful of whom she speaks to, and what she says. Let
the ward be a beauty, her confidante shall treat you
with an air of distance; let her be a fortune, and she
assumes the suspicious behavior of her friend and
patroness. Thus it is that very many of our unmar-
ried women of distinction are to all intents and pur-
poses married, except the consideration of different
sexes. They are directly under the conduct of their
whisperer; and think they are in a state of freedom,
while they can prate with one of these attendants of
all men in general and still avoid the man they most
like. You do not see one heiress in an hundred whose
fate does not turn upon this circumstance of choosing
a confidante. Thus it is that the lady is addressed
to, presented and flattered, only by proxy, in her
woman. In my case, how is it possible that — "

Sir Roger was proceeding in his harangue, when
we heard the voice of one speaking very importu-
nately, and repeating these words, "What, not one
smile?" We followed the sound till we came to a
close thicket, on the other side of which we saw a
young woman sitting as it were in a personated[2] sul-
lenness just over a transparent fountain. Opposite
to her stood Mr. William, Sir Roger's master of the
game. The Knight whispered me, "Hist, these are
lovers." The huntsman looking earnestly at the

1. Note below, "be a beauty," "be a fortune."
2. See a similar use of this word (p. 79, l. 3).

shadow of the young maiden in the stream, "O thou
dear picture, if thou couldst remain there in the
absence of that fair creature, whom you represent in
the water, how willingly could I stand here satisfied
forever, without troubling my dear Betty herself
with any mention of her unfortunate William, whom
she is angry with: but alas! when she pleases to be
gone, thou wilt also vanish — yet let me talk to thee
while thou dost stay. Tell my dearest Betty thou
dost not more depend upon her than does her William: her absence will make away with me as well as
thee. If she offers to remove thee, I'll jump into
these waves to lay hold on thee ; herself, her own
dear person, I must never embrace again. — Still do
you hear me without one smile — it is too much to
bear." He had no sooner spoke these words but
he made an offer of throwing himself into the water;
at which his mistress started up, and at the next instant he jumped across the fountain and met her in
an embrace. She, half recovering from her fright,
said in the most charming voice imaginable, and
with a tone of complaint, "I thought how well you
would drown yourself. No, no, you won't drown
yourself till you have taken your leave of Susan
Holiday." The huntsman, with a tenderness that
spoke the most passionate love, and with his cheek
close to hers, whispered the softest vows of fidelity
in her ear, and cried, "Don't, my dear, believe a
word Kate Willow says; she is spiteful and makes
stories, because she loves to hear me talk to herself
for your sake."

"Look you there," quoth Sir Roger, "do you see
there, all mischief comes from confidantes! But let
us not interrupt them; the maid is honest, and the

man dares not be otherwise, for he knows I loved her
father; I will interpose in this matter, and hasten
the wedding. Kate Willow is a witty mischievous
wench in the neighborhood, who was a beauty; and
makes me hope I shall see the perverse Widow in her
condition. She was so flippant with her answers to
all the honest fellows that came near her, and so very
vain of her beauty, that she has valued herself upon
her charms till they are ceased. She therefore now
makes it her business to prevent other young women
from being more discreet than she was herself; however, the saucy thing said the other day well enough,
'Sir Roger and I must make a match, for we are
both despised by those we loved.' The hussy has a
great deal of power wherever she comes, and has her
share of cunning.

"However, when I reflect upon this woman, I do
not know whether in the main I am the worse for
having loved her; whenever she is recalled to my
imagination my youth returns and I feel a forgotten
warmth in my veins. This affliction in my life has
streaked all my conduct with a softness of which I
should otherwise have been incapable. It is, perhaps, to this dear image in my heart owing, that I
am apt to relent, that I easily forgive, and that many
desirable things are grown into my temper, which I
should not have arrived at by better motives than the
thought of being one day hers. I am pretty well satisfied such a passion as I have had is never well
cured; and between you and me, I am often apt to
imagine it has had some whimsical effect upon my
brain. For I frequently find, that in my most serious discourse I let fall some comical familiarity of
speech or odd phrase that makes the company laugh;

however, I cannot but allow she is a most excellent woman. When she is in the country, I warrant she does not run into dairies, but reads upon the nature of plants; but has a glass hive, and comes into the garden out of books to see them work, and observe the policies of their commonwealth. She understands everything. I'd give ten pounds to hear her argue with my friend Sir Andrew Freeport about trade. No, no, for all she looks so innocent as it were, take my word for it she is no fool."

SIR ROGER DE COVERLEY.

XVIII. POLITE AND RUSTIC MANNERS.

Urbem quam dicunt Romam, Melibœe, putavi
Stultus ego huic nostrœ similem.[1]

VIRGIL, Eclogues, i. 20, 21.

THE first and most obvious reflections which arise
in a man who changes the city for the country[2] are
upon the different manners of the people whom he
meets with in those two different scenes of life. By
manners I do not mean morals, but behavior and
good-breeding as they show themselves in the town
and in the country.

And here, in the first place, I must observe a very

1.   The city, Melibœus, that men call Rome,
       I, silly, thought like my small town.

2. It must be remembered that when Addison wrote, the
infrequent intercourse between city and country left every petty
neighborhood to form its own manners and dress, almost its own
language. "A journey any little distance from home was a
serious undertaking, so serious, indeed, that it often meant the
inditing of a last will and testament before it was undertaken.
Bad as the roads were in the summer-time when clouds of dust
blinded the traveller in every direction, infinitely worse were
they at such times as the waters were out or after a heavy fall
of rain, when the chances were that wayfarers, after crawling
along at a pace of two or three miles an hour in constant fear of
sticking fast in a quagmire, had to brave the impetuous force of
the current of some river that had overflowed its banks, the
strong barely escaping with their lives, the weak often perishing
in the stream." — SYDNEY, *England and the English in the Eighteenth Century*, ii. 5.

great revolution that has happened in this article of good-breeding. Several obliging deferences, condescensions, and submissions, with many outward forms and ceremonies that accompany them, were first of all brought up among the politer part of mankind, who lived in courts and cities, and distinguished themselves from the rustic part of the species (who on all occasions acted bluntly and naturally) by such a mutual complaisance and intercourse of civilities. These forms of conversation by degrees multiplied and grew troublesome; the modish world found too great a constraint in them, and have therefore thrown most of them aside. Conversation, like the Romish religion, was so encumbered with show and ceremony, that it stood in need of a reformation to retrench its superfluities, and restore it to its natural good sense and beauty. At present therefore an unconstrained carriage, and a certain openness of behavior, are the height of good-breeding. The fashionable world is grown free and easy; our manners sit more loose upon us. Nothing is so modish as an agreeable negligence. In a word, good-breeding shows itself most, where to an ordinary eye it appears the least.

If after this we look on the people of mode in the country we find in them the manners of the last age. They have no sooner fetched themselves up to the fashion of the polite world, but the town has dropped them, and are nearer to the first state of nature than to those refinements which formerly reigned in the court, and still prevail in the country. One may now know a man that never conversed in the world by his excess of good-breeding. A polite country squire shall make you as many bows in half an hour as would serve a courtier for a week. There is infi-

nitely more to do about place and precedency in a
meeting of justices' wives than in an assembly of
duchesses.

This rural politeness is very troublesome to a man
of my temper, who generally take the chair that is
next me, and walk first or last, in the front or in the
rear, as chance directs. I have known my friend Sir
Roger's dinner almost cold before the company could
adjust the ceremonial, and be prevailed upon to sit
down; and have heartily pitied my old friend, when
I have seen him forced to pick and cull his guests, as
they sat at the several parts of his table, that he
might drink their healths according to their respective ranks and qualities. Honest Will Wimble,
who I should have thought had been altogether unin-
fected with ceremony, gives me abundance of trouble
in this particular. Though he has been fishing all
the morning, he will not help himself at dinner till I
am served. When we are going out of the hall, he
runs behind me; and last night, as we were walking
in the fields, stopped short at a stile till I came up to
it, and upon my making signs to him to get over,
told me, with a serious smile, that sure I believed
they had no manners in the country.

There has happened another revolution in the
point of good-breeding, which relates to the conversation among men of mode, and which I cannot but
look upon as very extraordinary. It was certainly
one of the first distinctions of a well-bred man, to
express everything that had the most remote appearance of being obscene in modest terms and distant
phrases; whilst the clown, who had no such delicacy
of conception and expression, clothed his ideas in
those plain, homely terms that are the most obvious

and natural. This kind of good manners was perhaps carried to an excess, so as to make conversation
too stiff, formal, and precise: for which reason (as
hypocrisy in one age is generally succeeded by athe-
ism in another) conversation is in a great measure
relapsed into the first extreme; so that at present
several of our men of the town, and particularly
those who have been polished in France, make use
of the most coarse uncivilized words in our language,
and utter themselves often in such a manner as a
clown would blush to hear.

This infamous piece of good-breeding, which reigns
among the coxcombs of the town, has not yet made
its way into the country; and as it is impossible for
such an irrational way of conversation to last long
among a people that make any profession of religion,
or show of modesty, if the country gentlemen get
into it they will certainly be left in the lurch. Their
good-breeding will come too late to them, and they
will be thought a parcel of lewd clowns, while they
fancy themselves talking together like men of wit
and pleasure.

As the two points of good-breeding which I have
hitherto insisted upon regard behavior and conversation, there is a third, which turns upon dress. In
this, too, the country are very much behind-hand.
The rural beaus are not yet got out of the fashion
that took place at the time of the Revolution, but
ride about the country in red coats and laced [1] hats,
while the women in many parts are still trying to
outvie one another in the height of their head-
dresses. [2]

1. That is, edged with gold lace.
2. About a month before Addison had written in *The Specta-*

But a friend of mine, who is now upon the western circuit, having promised to give me an account of the several modes and fashions that prevail in the different parts of the nation through which he passes, I shall defer the enlarging upon this last topic till I have received a letter from him, which I expect every post.

XIX. THE COVERLEY POULTRY.

Equidem credo, quia sit divinitus illis
Ingenium.[1]

VIRGIL, *Georgics*, i. 451.

My friend Sir Roger is very often merry with me upon my passing so much of my time among his poultry. He has caught me twice or thrice looking

tor, No. 98 : "There is not so variable a thing in nature as a lady's head-dress. Within my own memory I have known it rise and fall above thirty degrees. About thirty years ago it shot up to a very great height, insomuch that the female part of our species were much taller than the men. The women were of such an enormous stature that we appeared as grasshoppers before them. At present the whole sex is in a manner dwarfed and shrunk into a race of beauties that seems almost another species. I remember several ladies who were once very near seven foot high, that at present want some inches of five. . . . One may observe that women in all ages have taken more pains than men to adorn the outside of their heads ; and, indeed, I very much admire that those female architects who raise such wonderful structures out of ribbands, lace, and wire, have not been recorded for their respective inventions. It is certain there has been as many orders in these kinds of building as in those which have been made of marble ; sometimes they rise in the shape of a pyramid, sometimes like a tower, and sometimes like a steeple."

1. I verily believe that their intelligence has something divine about it.

after a bird's nest, and several times sitting an hour or two together near an hen and chickens.   He tells me he believes I am personally acquainted with every fowl about his house; calls such a particular cock my favorite, and frequently complains that his ducks and geese have more of my company than himself.

I must confess I am infinitely delighted with those speculations of nature which are to be made in a country life; and as my reading has very much lain among books of natural history, I cannot forbear recollecting upon this occasion the several remarks which I have met with in authors, and comparing them with what falls under my own observation: the arguments for Providence drawn from the natural history of animals being in my opinion demonstrative.

The make of every kind of animal is different from that of every other kind; and yet there is not the least turn in the muscles or twist in the fibres of any one, which does not render them more proper for that particular animal's way of life than any other cast or texture of them would have been.

The most violent appetites in all creatures are lust and hunger.   The first is a perpetual call upon them to propagate their kind; the latter to preserve themselves.

It is astonishing to consider the different degrees of care that descend from the parent to the young, so far as is absolutely necessary for the leaving a posterity.   Some creatures cast their eggs as chance directs them, and think of them no farther, as insects and several kinds of fish; others, of a nicer frame, find out proper beds to deposit them in, and there leave them, as the serpent, the crocodile, and ostrich; others hatch their eggs and tend the birth, till it is able to shift for itself.

What can we call the principle which directs every different kind of bird to observe a particular plan in the structure of its nest, and directs all of the same species to work after the same model? It cannot be imitation; for though you hatch a crow under a hen, and never let it see any of the works of its own kind, the nest it makes shall be the same, to the laying of a stick, with all the other nests of the same species. It cannot be reason; for were animals indued with it to as great a degree as man, their buildings would be as different as ours, according to the different conveniences that they would propose to themselves.

Is it not remarkable, that the same temper of weather, which raises this genial warmth in animals, should cover the trees with leaves, and the fields with grass, for their security and concealment, and produce such infinite swarms of insects for the support and sustenance of their respective broods?

Is it not wonderful that the love of the parent should be so violent while it lasts, and that it should last no longer than is necessary for the preservation of the young?

But notwithstanding this natural love in brutes is much more violent and intense than in rational creatures, Providence has taken care that it should be no longer troublesome to the parent than it is useful to the young ; for so soon as the wants of the latter cease, the mother withdraws her fondness, and leaves them to provide for themselves; and what is a very remarkable circumstance in this part of instinct, we find that the love of the parent may be lengthened out beyond its usual time, if the preservation of the species requires it: as we may see in birds that drive away their young as soon as they are able to get their livelihood, but continue to feed them if they are tied to the nest, or confined within a cage, or by any other means appear to be out of a condition of supplying their own necessities.

This natural love is not observed in animals to ascend from the young to the parent, which is not at all necessary for the continuance of the species: nor indeed in reasonable creatures does it rise in any proportion, as it spreads itself downwards; for in all family affection, we find protection granted and favors bestowed are greater motives to love and tenderness than safety, benefits, or life received.

One would wonder to hear skeptical men disputing for the reason of animals, and telling us it is only our pride and prejudices that will not allow them the use of that faculty.

Reason shows itself in all occurrences of life; whereas the brute makes no discovery of such a talent, but in what immediately regards his own preservation or the continuance of his species. Animals in their generation are wiser than the sons of men; but their wisdom is confined to a few particulars, and lies in a very narrow compass. Take a brute out of his instinct, and you find him wholly deprived of understanding. To use an instance that comes often under observation.

With what caution does the hen provide herself a nest in places unfrequented, and free from noise and disturbance! When she has laid her eggs in such a manner that she can cover them, what care does she take in turning them frequently, that all parts may partake of the vital warmth! When she leaves them, to provide for her necessary sustenance, how punctually does she return before they have time to cool, and become incapable of producing an animal! In the summer you see her giving herself greater freedoms, and quitting her care for above two hours together; but in winter, when the rigor of the season would chill the principles of life, and destroy the young one, she grows more assiduous in her attendance, and stays away but half the time. When the birth approaches, with how much nicety and attention does she help the chick to break its prison! not to take notice of her covering it from the injuries of the weather, providing it proper nourishment, and teaching it to help itself; nor to mention her forsaking the nest, if after the usual time of reckoning the young one does not make its appearance. A chemical operation could not be followed with greater art or diligence than is seen in the hatching of a chick; though there are many other birds that show an infinitely greater sagacity in all the fore-mentioned particulars.

But at the same time the hen, that has all this seeming ingenuity (which is indeed absolutely necessary for the propagation of the species), considered in other respects, is without the least glimmerings of thought or common sense. She mistakes a piece of chalk for an egg, and sits upon it in the same manner; she is insensible of any increase or diminution in the number of those she lays; she does not distinguish between her own and those of another species; and when the birth appears of never so different a bird, will cherish it for her own. In all these circumstances which do not carry an immediate regard to the subsistence of herself or her species, she is a very idiot.

There is not, in my opinion, anything more mysterious in nature than this instinct in animals, which thus rises above reason, and falls infinitely short of it. It cannot be accounted for by any properties in matter, and at the same time works after so odd a manner, that one cannot think it the faculty of an intellectual being. For my own part, I look upon it as upon the principle of gravitation in bodies, which is not to be explained by any known qualities inherent in the bodies themselves, nor from any laws of mechanism, but according to the best notions of the greatest philosophers is an immediate impression from the first Mover, and the Divine energy acting in the creatures.

XX. SIR ROGER IN THE COUNTRY.

Comes jucundus in via pro vehiculo est.[1]

PUBLIUS SYRUS, *Fragments.*

A MAN'S first care should be to avoid the reproaches of his own heart; his next to escape the censures of the world. If the last interferes with the former, it ought to be entirely neglected; but otherwise there cannot be a greater satisfaction to an honest mind than to see those approbations which it gives itself seconded by the applauses of the public. A man is more sure of his conduct when the verdict which he passes upon his own behavior is thus warranted and confirmed by the opinion of all that know him.

My worthy friend Sir Roger is one of those who is not only at peace within himself, but beloved and esteemed by all about him. He receives a suitable

1. A cheerful companion on the road is as good as a coach.

tribute for his universal benevolence to mankind in
the returns of affection and good-will which are paid
him by every one that lives within his neighborhood.
I lately met with two or three odd instances of that
general respect which is shown to the good old
Knight. He would needs carry Will Wimble and
myself with him to the county assizes. As we were
upon the road, Will Wimble joined a couple of plain
men who rid before us, and conversed with them for
some time; during which my friend Sir Roger acquainted me with their characters.

"The first of them," says he, "that has a spaniel
by his side, is a yeoman of about an hundred pounds
a year, an honest man. He is just within the Game
Act, and qualified to kill an hare or a pheasant. He
knocks down a dinner with his gun twice or thrice a
week; and by that means lives much cheaper than
those who have not so good an estate as himself. He
would be a good neighbor if he did not destroy so
many partridges; in short, he is a very sensible man,
shoots flying, and has been several times foreman of
the petty jury.

"The other that rides along with him is Tom
Touchy, a fellow famous for taking the law of everybody. There is not one in the town where he lives
that he has not sued at a quarter sessions. The
rogue had once the impudence to go to law with the
Widow. His head is full of costs, damages, and
ejectments; he plagued a couple of honest gentlemen
so long for a trespass in breaking one of his hedges,
till he was forced to sell the ground it enclosed to
defray the charges of the prosecution. His father
left him four-score pounds a year, but he has cast,[1]

1. Condemned in a lawsuit.

and been cast so often, that he is not now worth thirty. I suppose he is going upon the old business of the willow tree."

As Sir Roger was giving me this account of Tom Touchy, Will Wimble and his two companions stopped short till we came up to them. After having paid their respects to Sir Roger, Will told him that Mr. Touchy and he must appeal to him upon a dispute that arose between them. Will, it seems, had been giving his fellow traveller an account of his angling one day in such a hole; when Tom Touchy, instead of hearing out his story, told him that Mr. Such-an-one, if he pleased, might take the law of him for fishing in that part of the river. My friend Sir Roger heard them both, upon a round trot; and, after having paused some time, told them, with the air of a man who would not give his judgment rashly, that much might be said on both sides. They were neither of them dissatisfied with the Knight's determination, because neither of them found himself in the wrong by it. Upon which we made the best of our way to the assizes.

The court was sat before Sir Roger came; but notwithstanding all the justices had taken their places upon the bench, they made room for the old Knight at the head of them; who, for his reputation in the country, took occasion to whisper in the judge's ear, that he was glad his lordship had met with so much good weather in his circuit. I was listening to the proceeding of the court with much attention, and infinitely pleased with that great appearance and solemnity which so properly accompanies such a public administration of our laws; when, after about an hour's sitting, I observed, to my great surprise, in the midst of a trial, that my friend Sir Roger was getting up to speak. I was in some pain for him, till I found he had acquitted himself of two or three sentences, with a look of much business and great intrepidity.

Upon his first rising the court was hushed, and a general whisper ran among the country people that Sir Roger was up. The speech he made was so little to the purpose, that I shall not trouble my readers with an account of it; and I believe was not so much designed by the Knight himself to inform the court, as to give him a figure in my eye, and keep up his credit in the country.

I was highly delighted, when the court rose, to see the gentlemen of the country gathering about my old friend, and striving who should compliment him most; at the same time that the ordinary people gazed upon him at a distance, not a little admiring his courage, that was not afraid to speak to the judge.

In our return home we met with a very odd accident, which I cannot forbear relating, because it shows how desirous all who know Sir Roger are of giving him marks of their esteem. When we were arrived upon the verge of his estate, we stopped at a little inn to rest ourselves and our horses. The man of the house had, it seems, been formerly a servant in the Knight's family; and, to do honor to his old master, had some time since, unknown to Sir Roger, put him up in a sign-post before the door; so that the Knight's Head had hung out upon the road about a week before he himself knew anything of the matter. As soon as Sir Roger was acquainted with it, finding that his servant's indiscretion proceeded

wholly from affection and good-will, he only told him
that he had made him too high a compliment; and
when the fellow seemed to think that could hardly
be, added, with a more decisive look, that it was too
great an honor for any man under a duke; but told
him at the same time that it might be altered with
a very few touches, and that he himself would be at
the charge of it. Accordingly they got a painter, by
the Knight's directions, to add a pair of whiskers to
the face, and by a little aggravation of the features
to change it into the Saracen's Head.[1] I should not
have known this story had not the inn-keeper, upon
Sir Roger's alighting, told him in my hearing, that
his honor's head was brought back last night with
the alterations that he had ordered to be made in it.
Upon this, my friend, with his usual cheerfulness,
related the particulars above mentioned, and ordered
the head to be brought into the room. I could not
forbear discovering greater expressions of mirth than
ordinary upon the appearance of this monstrous face,
under which, notwithstanding it was made to frown
and stare in a most extraordinary manner, I could
still discover a distant resemblance of my old friend.
Sir Roger, upon seeing me laugh, desired me to tell
him truly if I thought it possible for people to know
him in that disguise. I at first kept my usual silence; but upon the Knight's conjuring me to tell
him whether it was not still more like himself than a
Saracen, I composed my countenance in the best

1. "When our countrymen came home from fighting with the
Saracens, and were beaten by them, they pictured them with
huge, big, terrible faces (as you still see the sign of the Saracen's Head is), when, in truth, they were like other men. But
this they did to save their own credit." — SELDEN's *Table Talk.*

manner I could, and replied that much might be said on both sides.

These several adventures, with the Knight's behavior in them, gave me as pleasant a day as ever I met with in any of my travels.

XXI. FLORIO AND LEONILLA.

Doctrina sed vim promovet insitam
Rectique cultus pectora roborant;
Utcunque defecere mores,
Dedecorant bene nata culpæ.[1]

HORACE, *Ode iv. 4, 33.*

As I was yesterday taking the air with my friend Sir Roger, we were met by a fresh-colored ruddy young man, who rid by us full speed, with a couple of servants behind him. Upon my inquiry who he was, Sir Roger told me that he was a young gentleman of a considerable estate, who had been educated by a tender mother, that lives not many miles from the place where we were. She is a very good lady, says my friend, but took so much care of her son's health, that she has made him good for nothing. She quickly found that reading was bad for his eyes, and that writing made his head ache. He was let loose among the woods as soon as he was able to ride on horseback, or to carry a gun upon his shoulder. To be brief, I found by my friend's account of him,

1. Instruction a new force imparts
   To faculties inherited,
   And, well directed, strengthens hearts
   In virtue's ways and valor's bred;
   But when bad morals bring bad fame,
   Good birth but aggravates the shame.
                    John O. Sargent's translation.

that he had got a great stock of health, but nothing
else; and that if it were a man's business only to
live, there would not be a more accomplished young
fellow in the whole country.

The truth of it is, since my residing in these parts
I have seen and heard innumerable instances of
young heirs and elder brothers who either from their
own reflecting upon the estates they are born to, and
therefore thinking all other accomplishments unnecessary, or from hearing these notions frequently inculcated to them by the flattery of their servants and
domestics, or from the same foolish thought prevail-
ing in those who have the care of their education, are
of no manner of use but to keep up their families,
and transmit their lands and houses in a line to posterity.

This makes me often think on a story I have heard
of two friends, which I shall give my reader at large
under feigned names. The moral of it may, I hope,
be useful, though there are some circumstances which
make it rather appear like a novel [1] than a true story.

Eudoxus and Leontine began the world with small
estates. They were both of them men of good sense
and great virtue. They prosecuted their studies together in their earlier years, and entered into such a
friendship as lasted to the end of their lives. Eudoxus, at his first setting out in the world, threw
himself into a court, where by his natural endowments and his acquired abilities he made his way
from one post to another, till at length he had raised
a very considerable fortune. Leontine, on the con-

---

1. The novel as understood by Addison was a short story with
love for its motive. Novels of this character were often introduced into papers like *The Spectator*.

trary, sought all opportunities of improving his mind by study, conversation, and travel. He was not only acquainted with all the sciences, but with the most eminent professors of them throughout Europe. He knew perfectly well the interests of its princes, with the customs and fashions of their courts, and could scarce meet with the name of an extraordinary person in the Gazette whom he had not either talked to or seen. In short, he had so well mixed and digested his knowledge of men and books, that he made one of the most accomplished persons of his age. During the whole course of his studies and travels he kept up a punctual correspondence with Eudoxus, who often made himself acceptable to the principal men about court by the intelligence which he received from Leontine. When they were both turned of forty (an age in which, according to Mr. Cowley,[1] "there is no dallying with life") they determined, pursuant to the resolution they had taken in the beginning of their lives, to retire, and pass the remainder of their days in the country. In order to this, they both of them married much about the same time. Leontine, with his own and his wife's fortune, bought a farm of three hundred a year, which lay within the neighborhood of his friend Eudoxus, who had purchased an estate of as many thousands. They were both of them fathers about the same time, Eudoxus having a son born to him, and Leontine a daughter; but to the unspeakable grief of the latter, his young wife, in whom all his happiness was wrapt up, died in a few days after the birth of her daugh-

---

1. From Cowley's *Essay on the Danger of Procrastination*, in which occurs the phrase, "There's no fooling with life when it is once turned beyond forty."

ter. His affliction would have been insupportable, had not he been comforted by the daily visits and conversations of his friend. As they were one day talking together with their usual intimacy, Leontine considering how incapable he was of giving his daughter a proper education in his own house, and Eudoxus reflecting on the ordinary behavior of a son who knows himself to be the heir of a great estate, they both agreed upon an exchange of children, namely, that the boy should be bred up with Leontine as his son, and that the girl should live with Eudoxus as his daughter, till they were each of them arrived at years of discretion. The wife of Eudoxus, knowing that her son could not be so advantageously brought up as under the care of Leontine, and considering at the same time that he would be perpetually under her own eye, was by degrees prevailed upon to fall in with the project. She therefore took Leonilla, for that was the name of the girl, and educated her as her own daughter. The two friends on each side had wrought themselves to such an habitual tenderness for the children who were under their direction, that each of them had the real passion of a father, where the title was but imaginary. Florio, the name of the young heir that lived with Leontine, though he had all the duty and affection imaginable for his supposed parent, was taught to rejoice at the sight of Eudoxus, who visited his friend very frequently, and was dictated by his natural affection, as well as by the rules of prudence, to make himself esteemed and beloved by Florio. The boy was now old enough to know his supposed father's circumstances, and that therefore he was to make his way in the world by his own industry. This considera-

tion grew stronger in him every day, and produced
so good an effect that he applied himself with more
than ordinary attention to the pursuit of everything
which Leontine recommended to him. His natural
abilities, which were very good, assisted by the
directions of so excellent a counsellor, enabled him
to make a quicker progress than ordinary through all
the parts of his education. Before he was twenty
years of age, having finished his studies and exercises
with great applause, he was removed from the university to the inns of court, where there are very few
that make themselves considerable proficients in the
studies of the place who know they shall arrive at
great estates without them. This was not Florio's
case; he found that three hundred a year was but a
poor estate for Leontine and himself to live upon, so
that he studied without intermission till he gained a
very good insight into the constitution and laws of
his country.

I should have told my reader that whilst Florio
lived at the house of his foster-father he was always
an acceptable guest in the family of Eudoxus, where
he became acquainted with Leonilla from her infancy. His acquaintance with her by degrees grew
into love, which in a mind trained up in all the sentiments of honor and virtue became a very uneasy
passion. He despaired of gaining an heiress of so
great a fortune, and would rather have died than
attempted it by any indirect methods. Leonilla,
who was a woman of the greatest beauty joined with
the greatest modesty, entertained at the same time a
secret passion for Florio, but conducted herself with
so much prudence that she never gave him the least
intimation of it. Florio was now engaged in all

those arts and improvements that are proper to raise
a man's private fortune, and give him a figure in his
country, but secretly tormented with that passion
which burns with the greatest fury in a virtuous and
noble heart, when he received a sudden summons
from Leontine to repair to him into the country the
next day. For it seems Eudoxus was so filled with
the report of his son's reputation, that he could no
longer withhold making himself known to him. The
morning after his arrival at the house of his supposed
father, Leontine told him that Eudoxus had something of great importance to communicate to him;
upon which the good man embraced him and wept.
Florio was no sooner arrived at the great house that
stood in his neighborhood, but Eudoxus took him by
the hand, after the first salutes were over, and conducted him into his closet. He there opened to him
the whole secret of his parentage and education, concluding after this manner: "I have no other way left
of acknowledging my gratitude to Leontine, than by
marrying you to his daughter. He shall not lose the
pleasure of being your father by the discovery I have
made to you. Leonilla, too, shall be still my daughter; her filial piety, though misplaced, has been so
exemplary that it deserves the greatest reward I can
confer upon it. You shall have the pleasure of seeing a great estate fall to you, which you would have
lost the relish of had you known yourself born to it.
Continue only to deserve it in the same manner you
did before you were possessed of it. I have left your
mother in the next room. Her heart yearns towards
you. She is making the same discoveries to Leonilla
which I have made to yourself." Florio was so over-
whelmed with this profusion of happiness, that he

was not able to make a reply, but threw himself
down at his father's feet, and amidst a flood of tears
kissed and embraced his knees, asking his blessing,
and expressing in dumb show those sentiments of
love, duty, and gratitude that were too big for utter-
ance. To conclude, the happy pair were married,
and half Eudoxus's estate settled upon them. Leontine and Eudoxus passed the remainder of their lives
together; and received in the dutiful and affectionate
behavior of Florio and Leonilla the just recompense,
as well as the natural effects, of that care which they
had bestowed upon them in their education.[1]

XXII. SIR ROGER AND PARTY SPIRIT.

Ne, pueri, ne tanta animis assuescite bella :
Neu patriæ validas in viscera vertite vires.[2]
VIRGIL, *Æneid*, vi. 832, 833.

My worthy friend Sir Roger, when we are talking
of the malice of parties, very frequently tells us an
accident that happened to him when he was a school-
boy, which was at a time when the feuds ran high
between the Roundheads and Cavaliers. This worthy

1. Addison writing to Mr. Wortley (afterward Wortley Mon-
tague) on the day when this number of *The Spectator* appeared,
says : "Being very well pleased with this day's *Spectator*, I cannot forbear sending you one of them, and desiring your opinion
of the story in it. When you have a son, I shall be glad to be
his Leontine, as my circumstances will be like his. I have
within this twelvemonth lost a place of £2,000 per annum, an
estate in the Indies of £14,000, and what is worse than all the
rest, my mistress." Addison had been in vain suing for the
hand of a "perverse widow," who had now finally rejected him.
2.   Children, become not wonted to so great a war,
    Nor turn your energies into rending your country.

Knight, being then but a stripling, had occasion to inquire which was the way to St. Anne's Lane, upon which the person whom he spoke to, instead of answering his question, called him a young Popish cur, and asked him who had made Anne a saint! The boy, being in some confusion, inquired of the next he met, which was the way to Anne's Lane; but was called a prick-eared cur for his pains, and instead of being shown the way, was told that she had been a saint before he was born, and would be one after he was hanged. "Upon this," says Sir Roger, "I did not think fit to repeat the former question, but going into every lane of the neighborhood, asked what they called the name of that lane." By which ingenious artifice he found out the place he inquired after, without giving offence to any party. Sir Roger generally closes this narrative with reflections on the mischief that parties do in the country; how they spoil good neighborhood, and make honest gentlemen hate one another; besides that they manifestly tend to the prejudice of the land tax,[1] and the destruction of the game.

There cannot a greater judgment befall a country than such a dreadful spirit of division as rends a government into two distinct people, and makes them greater strangers and more averse to one another, than if they were actually two different nations. The effects of such a division are pernicious to the last degree, not only with regard to those advantages which they give the common enemy, but to those private evils which they produce in the heart of almost every particular person. This influence is

1. For the origin of the land tax see Macaulay's *History of England*, chap. ii.

very fatal both to men's morals and their understandings; it sinks the virtue of a nation, and not
only so, but destroys even common sense.

A furious party spirit, when it rages in its full
violence, exerts itself in civil war and bloodshed;
and when it is under its greatest restraints naturally
breaks out in falsehood, detraction, calumny, and a
partial administration of justice. In a word, it fills
a nation with spleen and rancor, and extinguishes
all the seeds of good-nature, compassion, and humanity.[1]

Plutarch says, very finely, "that a man should not
allow himself to hate even his enemies, because," says
he, "if you indulge this passion in some occasions,
it will rise of itself in others; if you hate your enemies, you will contract such a vicious habit of mind,
as by degrees will break out upon those who are
your friends, or those who are indifferent to you."
I might here observe how admirably this precept of
morality (which derives the malignity of hatred from
the passion itself, and not from its object) answers to
that great rule which was dictated to the world about
an hundred years before this philosopher wrote;[2] but
instead of that, I shall only take notice, with a real
grief of heart, that the minds of many good men

1. It is generally recognized that party spirit never raged in
England as in the eighteenth century. The cause lies deep in
history, but the spirit of partisanship was intensified as well as
in a measure due to the seat of power which was not so much in
organization as in persons and families. The old feudal conditions had given way ; the new conditions of administration by
parliament had not yet become fixed ; meanwhile the feudal
spirit remained, but found its exercise in politics and society,
rather than in war.

2. Luke vi. 27–32.

among us appear soured with party-principles, and alienated from one another in such a manner, as seems to me altogether inconsistent with the dictates either of reason or religion. Zeal for a public cause is apt to breed passions in the hearts of virtuous persons, to which the regard of their own private interest would never have betrayed them.

If this party spirit has so ill an effect on our morals, it has likewise a very great one upon our judgments. We often hear a poor insipid paper or pamphlet cried up, and sometimes a noble piece depreciated, by those who are of a different principle from the author. One who is actuated by this spirit is almost under an incapacity of discerning either real blemishes or beauties. A man of merit in a different principle is like an object seen in two different mediums, that appears crooked or broken, however straight and entire it may be in itself. For this reason there is scarce a person of any figure in England who does not go by two contrary characters, as opposite to one another as light and darkness. Knowledge and learning suffer in a particular manner from this strange prejudice, which at present prevails amongst all ranks and degrees in the British nation. As men formerly became eminent in learned societies by their parts and acquisitions, they now distinguish themselves by the warmth and violence with which they espouse their respective parties. Books are valued upon the like considerations. An abusive, scurrilous style passes for satire, and a dull scheme of party notions is called fine writing.

There is one piece of sophistry practised by both sides, and that is the taking any scandalous story, that has been ever whispered or invented of a private man, for a known undoubted truth, and raising suitable speculations upon it. Calumnies that have been never proved, or have been often refuted, are the ordinary postulatums of these infamous scribblers, upon which they proceed as upon first principles granted by all men, though in their hearts they know they are false, or at best very doubtful. When they have laid these foundations of scurrility, it is no wonder that their superstructure is every way answerable to them. If this shameless practice of the present age endures much longer, praise and reproach will cease to be motives of action in good men.

There are certain periods of time in all governments when this inhuman spirit prevails. Italy was long torn in pieces by the Guelphs and Ghibellines, and France by those who were for and against the league:[1] but it is very unhappy for a man to be born in such a stormy and tempestuous season. It is the restless ambition of artful men that thus breaks a people into factions, and draws several well-meaning persons to their interest by a specious concern for their country. How many honest minds are filled with uncharitable and barbarous notions, out of their zeal for the public good? What cruelties and outrages would they not commit against men of an adverse party, whom they would honor and esteem, if, instead of considering them as they are represented, they knew them as they are? Thus are persons of the greatest probity seduced into shameful errors and prejudices, and made bad men even by that noblest of principles, the love of their country. I

1. The Catholic League, so called, headed by the Duke of Guise, whose purpose was to insure the succession of a Catholic to the crown after the death of Henri III. of France.

cannot here forbear mentioning the famous Spanish proverb, "If there were neither fools nor knaves in the world, all people would be of one mind."

For my own part I could heartily wish that all honest men would enter into an association, for the support of one another against the endeavors of those whom they ought to look upon as their common enemies, whatsoever side they may belong to. Were there such an honest body of neutral forces, we should never see the worst of men in great figures of life, because they are useful to a party; nor the best unregarded, because they are above practising those methods which would be grateful to their faction. We should then single every criminal out of the herd, and hunt him down, however formidable and overgrown he might appear; on the contrary, we should shelter distressed innocence, and defend virtue, however beset with contempt or ridicule, envy or defamation. In short, we should not any longer regard our fellow-subjects as Whigs or Tories, but should make the man of merit our friend, and the villain our enemy.

XXIII. SIR ROGER AND POLITICS.

Tros Rutulusve fuat, nullo discrimine habebo.[1]

VIRGIL, *Æneid*, x. 108.

IN my yesterday's paper I proposed that the honest men of all parties should enter into a kind of association for the defence of one another, and the confusion of their common enemies. As it is designed this neutral body should act with a regard to

1. Be he Trojan or Rutulian, I 'll treat him all the same.

nothing but truth and equity, and divest themselves
of the little heats and prepossessions that cleave to
parties of all kinds, I have prepared for them the
following form of an association, which may express
their intentions in the most plain and simple manner.

*We, whose names are hereunto subscribed, do sol-
emnly declare, that we do in our consciences believe
two and two make four ; and that we shall adjudge
any man whatsoever to be our enemy who endeavors
to persuade us to the contrary. We are likewise
ready to maintain, with the hazard of all that is near
and dear to us, that six is less than seven in all times
and all places ; and that ten will not be more three
years hence than it is at present. We do also firmly
declare, that it is our resolution as long as we live to
call black black, and white white. And we shall
upon all occasions oppose such persons that upon any
day of the year shall call black white, or white black,
with the utmost peril of our lives and fortunes.*

Were there such a combination of honest men,
who without any regard to places would endeavor to
extirpate all such furious zealots as would sacrifice
one half of their country to the passion and interest
of the other; as also such infamous hypocrites, that
are for promoting their own advantage under color
of the public good; with all the profligate immoral
retainers to each side, that have nothing to recommend them but an implicit submission to their lead-
ers, we should soon see that furious party-spirit
extinguished, which may in time expose us to the
derision and contempt of all the nations about us.

A member of this society that would thus carefully
employ himself in making room for merit, by throwing down the worthless and depraved part of man-

kind from those conspicuous stations of life to which they have been sometimes advanced, and all this without any regard to his private interest, would be no small benefactor to his country.

I remember to have read in Diodorus Siculus an account of a very active little animal, which I think he calls the ichneumon, that makes it the whole business of his life to break the eggs of the crocodile, which he is always in search after. This instinct is the more remarkable, because the ichneumon never feeds upon the eggs he has broken, nor in any other way finds his account in them. Were it not for the incessant labors of this industrious animal, Egypt, says the historian, would be overrun with crocodiles; for the Egyptians are so far from destroying those pernicious creatures, that they worship them as gods.

If we look into the behavior of ordinary partisans, we shall find them far from resembling this disinterested animal; and rather acting after the example of the wild Tartars, who are ambitious of destroying a man of the most extraordinary parts and accomplishments, as thinking that upon his decease the same talents, whatever post they qualified him for, enter of course into his destroyer.

As in the whole train of my speculations I have endeavored, as much as I am able, to extinguish that pernicious spirit of passion and prejudice which rages with the same violence in all parties, I am still the more desirous of doing some good in this particular because I observe that the spirit of party reigns more in the country than in the town. It here contracts a kind of brutality and rustic fierceness, to which men of a politer conversation are wholly strangers. It extends itself even to the return of the bow and the hat; and at the same time that the heads of parties preserve toward one another an outward show of good-breeding, and keep up a perpetual intercourse of civilities, their tools that are dispersed in these outlying parts will not so much as mingle together at a cock-match.[1] This humor fills the country with several periodical meetings of Whig jockeys and Tory foxhunters, not to mention the innumerable curses, frowns, and whispers it produces at a quarter-sessions.

I do not know whether I have observed in any of my former papers, that my friends Sir Roger de Coverley and Sir Andrew Freeport are of different principles, the first of them inclined to the landed and the other to the moneyed interest. This humor is so moderate in each of them, that it proceeds no farther than to an agreeable raillery, which very often diverts the rest of the club. I find, however, that the Knight is a much stronger Tory in the country than in town, which, as he has told me in my ear, is absolutely necessary for the keeping up his interest. In all our journey from London to his house we did not so much as bait at a Whig inn; or if by chance the coachman stopped at a wrong place, one of Sir Roger's servants would ride up to his master full speed, and whisper to him that the master of the house was against such an one in the last election. This often betrayed us into hard beds and bad cheer; for we were not so inquisitive about the inn as the inn-keeper; and, provided our landlord's principles

---

1. In the humorous *Memoirs of P. P., Clerk of this Parish,* there is one Robert Jenkins, a Tory farrier, "a man of bright parts and shrewd conceit," who "never shoed a horse of a Whig or a fanatic but he lamed him sorely."

were sound, did not take any notice of the staleness of his provisions. This I found still the more inconvenient, because the better the host was, the worse generally were his accommodations; the fellow knowing very well that those who were his friends would take up with coarse diet and an hard lodging. For these reasons, all the while I was upon the road I dreaded entering into an house of any one that Sir Roger had applauded for an honest man.

Since my stay at Sir Roger's in the country, I daily find more instances of this narrow party-humor. Being upon a bowling-green at a neighboring market-town the other day (for that is the place where the gentlemen of one side meet once a week), I observed a stranger among them of a better presence and genteeler behavior than ordinary; but was much surprised, that notwithstanding he was a very fair better, nobody would take him up. But upon inquiry I found that he was one who had given a disagreeable vote in a former parliament, for which reason there was not a man upon that bowling-green who would have so much correspondence with him as to win his money of him.

Among other instances of this nature, I must not omit one which concerns myself. Will Wimble was the other day relating several strange stories that he had picked up, nobody knows where, of a certain great man; and upon my staring at him, as one that was surprised to hear such things in the country, which had never been so much as whispered in the town, Will stopped short in the thread of his discourse, and after dinner asked my friend Sir Roger in his ear if he was sure that I was not a fanatic.

It gives me a serious concern to see a spirit of

dissension in the country; not only as it destroys virtue and common sense, and renders us in a manner barbarians towards one another, but as it perpetuates our animosities, widens our breaches, and transmits our present passions and prejudices to our posterity. For my own part, I am sometimes afraid that I discover the seeds of a civil war in these our divisions; and therefore cannot but bewail, as in their first principles, the miseries and calamities of our children.[1]

XXIV. SIR ROGER AND THE GYPSIES.

Semperque recentes
Convectare juvat prædas, et vivere rapto.[2]
VIRGIL, *Æneid*, vii. 748.

As I was yesterday riding out in the fields with my friend Sir Roger, we saw at a little distance from us a troop of gypsies. Upon the first discovery of

1. The next day Addison began *The Spectator* with a passage which adds so agreeable a touch to the portrait of Sir Roger, that we copy it here, though the entire paper need not be included in a collection of *Sir Roger de Coverley Papers.* "It is our custom at Sir Roger's, upon the coming in of the post, to sit about a pot of coffee, and hear the old Knight read *Dyer's Letter ;* which he does with his spectacles upon his nose, and in an audible voice, smiling very often at those little strokes of satire, which are so frequent in the writings of that author. I afterwards communicate to the knight such packets as I receive under the quality of SPECTATOR. The following letter chancing to please him more than ordinary, I shall publish it at his request." The fiction of a visit at Sir Roger's country seat is preserved in the next paper still by a reference to certain characters living in Sir Roger's neighborhood.

2. Hunting their sport, and plundering was their trade.
DRYDEN.

them, my friend was in some doubt whether he
should not exert the justice of the peace upon such a
band of lawless vagrants; but not having his clerk
with him, who is a necessary counsellor on these
occasions, and fearing that his poultry might fare
the worse for it, he let the thought drop: but at the
same time gave me a particular account of the mis-
chiefs they do in the country, in stealing people's
goods and spoiling their servants. "If a stray piece
of linen hangs upon an hedge," says Sir Roger, "they
are sure to have it; if the hog loses his way in the
fields, it is ten to one but he becomes their prey; our
geese cannot live in peace for them; if a man pros-
ecutes them with severity, his hen-roost is sure to
pay for it: they generally straggle into these parts
about this time of the year; and set the heads of our
servant-maids so agog for husbands, that we do not
expect to have any business done as it should be
whilst they are in the country. I have an honest
dairy-maid who crosses their hands with a piece of
silver every summer, and never fails being promised
the handsomest young fellow in the parish for her
pains. Your friend the butler has been fool enough
to be seduced by them; and, though he is sure to lose
a knife, a fork, or a spoon every time his fortune is
told him, generally shuts himself up in the pantry
with an old gypsy for above half an hour once in a
twelvemonth. Sweethearts are the things they live
upon, which they bestow very plentifully upon all
those that apply themselves to them. You see now
and then some handsome young jades among them:
the sluts have very often white teeth and black eyes."

Sir Roger, observing that I listened with great
attention to his account of a people who were so

entirely new to me, told me that if I would they
should tell us our fortunes. As I was very well
pleased with the Knight's proposal, we rid up and
communicated our hands to them. A Cassandra of
the crew, after having examined my lines very diligently, told me that I loved a pretty maid in a corner; that I was a good woman's man; with some
other particulars which I do not think proper to
relate. My friend Sir Roger alighted from his
horse, and exposing his palm to two or three that
stood by him, they crumpled it into all shapes, and
diligently scanned every wrinkle that could be made
in it; when one of them, who was older and more
sunburnt than the rest, told him that he had a widow
in his line of life:[1] upon which the Knight cried,
"Go, go, you are an idle baggage;" and at the same
time smiled upon me. The gypsy, finding he was not
displeased in his heart, told him, after a farther inquiry into his hand, that his true love was constant,
and that she should dream of him to-night: my old
friend cried "Pish!" and bid her go on. The gypsy
told him that he was a bachelor, but would not be so
long; and that he was dearer to somebody than he
thought. The Knight still repeated she was an idle
baggage and bid her go on. "Ah, master," said the
gypsy, "that roguish leer of yours makes a pretty
woman's heart ache: you ha'n't that simper about
the mouth for nothing ——." The uncouth gibberish
with which all this was uttered, like the darkness of
an oracle, made us the more attentive to it. To be
short, the Knight left the money with her that he
had crossed her hand with, and got up again on his
horse.

1. The term given in palmistry to the principal line of the
hand.

As we were riding away, Sir Roger told me that he knew several sensible people who believed these gypsies now and then foretold very strange things; and for half an hour together appeared more jocund than ordinary. In the height of his good humor, meeting a common beggar upon the road who was no conjurer, as he went to relieve him he found his pocket was picked; that being a kind of palmistry at which this race of vermin are very dexterous.

I might here entertain my reader with historical remarks on this idle profligate people, who infest all the countries of Europe, and live in the midst of governments in a kind of commonwealth by themselves. But instead of entering into observations of this nature, I shall fill the remaining part of my paper with a story which is still fresh in Holland, and was printed in one of our monthly accounts about twenty years ago. "As the *trekschuyt*, or hackney-boat, which carries passengers from Leyden to Amsterdam, was putting off, a boy running along the side of the canal desired to be taken in: which the master of the boat refused, because the lad had not quite money enough to pay the usual fare. An eminent merchant being pleased with the looks of the boy, and secretly touched with compassion towards him, paid the money for him,[1] and ordered him to be taken on board. Upon talking with him afterwards, he found that he could speak readily in three or four languages, and learned upon farther examination that he had been stolen away when he was a child by a gypsy, and had rambled ever since with a gang of those strollers up and down several parts of Europe. It happened that the merchant, whose heart seems to

1. Hardly more than threepence English. — ADDISON.

have inclined towards the boy by a secret kind of instinct, had himself lost a child some years before. The parents, after a long search for him, gave him for drowned in one of the canals with which that country abounds; and the mother was so afflicted at the loss of a fine boy, who was her only son, that she died for grief of it. Upon laying together all particulars, and examining the several moles and marks by which the mother used to describe the child when he was first missing, the boy proved to be the son of the merchant, whose heart had so unaccountably melted at the sight of him. The lad was very well pleased to find a father who was so rich, and likely to leave him a good estate: the father on the other hand was not a little delighted to see a son return to him, whom he had given for lost, with such a strength of constitution, sharpness of understanding, and skill in languages." Here the printed story leaves off; but if I may give credit to reports, our linguist having received such extraordinary rudiments towards a good education, was afterwards trained up in everything that becomes a gentleman; wearing off by little and little all the vicious habits and practices that he had been used to in the course of his peregrinations. Nay, it is said that he has since been employed in foreign courts upon national business, with great reputation to himself and honor to those who sent him, and that he has visited several countries as a public minister, in which he formerly wandered as a gypsy.

XXV. THE SPECTATOR ENDS HIS VISIT TO COVERLEY HALL.

Ipsæ rursum concedite sylvæ.[1]

VIRGIL, *Eclogues*, x. 63.

IT is usual for a man who loves country sports to preserve the game in his own grounds, and divert himself upon those that belong to his neighbor. My friend Sir Roger generally goes two or three miles from his house, and gets into the frontiers of his estate, before he beats about in search of a hare or partridge, on purpose to spare his own fields, where he is always sure of finding diversion when the worst comes to the worst. By this means the breed about his house has time to increase and multiply; besides that the sport is the more agreeable where the game is the harder to come at, and where it does not lie so thick as to produce any perplexity or confusion in the pursuit. For these reasons the country gentleman, like the fox, seldom preys near his own home.

In the same manner I have made a month's excursion out of the town, which is the great field of game for sportsmen of my species, to try my fortune in the country, where I have started several subjects, and hunted them down, with some pleasure to myself, and I hope to others. I am here forced to use a great deal of diligence before I can spring anything to my mind; whereas in town, whilst I am following one character, it is ten to one but I am crossed in my way by another, and put up such a variety of odd creatures in both sexes, that they foil the scent of one another, and puzzle the chase. My greatest

1. "Once more, ye woods, adieu."

difficulty in the country is to find sport, and, in town, to choose it. In the mean time, as I have given a whole month's rest to the cities [1] of London and Westminster, I promise myself abundance of new game upon my return thither.

It is indeed high time for me to leave the country, since I find the whole neighborhood begin to grow very inquisitive after my name and character; my love of solitude, taciturnity, and particular way of life having raised a great curiosity in all these parts.

The notions which have been framed of me are various: some look upon me as very proud, some as very modest, and some as very melancholy. Will Wimble, as my friend the butler tells me, observing me very much alone, and extremely silent when I am in company, is afraid I have killed a man. The country people seem to suspect me for a conjurer; and, some of them hearing of the visit which I made to Moll White, will needs have it that Sir Roger has brought down a cunning man with him, to cure the old woman, and free the country from her charms. So that the character which I go under in part of the neighborhood is what they here call a "White Witch." [2]

1. In English law a city is the capital of a diocese, and for a brief time in the middle of the sixteenth century Westminster Abbey was a cathedral, and Westminster became a city. It did not resign its privileges when the bishopric was suppressed, and remained a city. In Addison's time the two cities were less compactly one than now ; the boundary was marked on the main thoroughfare by Temple Bar where the Strand met Fleet Street.

2. " According to popular belief, there were three classes of witches, — white, black, and gray. The first helped, but could not hurt ; the second the reverse ; and the third did both. White spirits caused stolen goods to be restored ; they charmed

A justice of peace, who lives about five miles off, and is not of Sir Roger's party, has, it seems, said twice or thrice at his table, that he wishes Sir Roger does not harbor a Jesuit in his house, and that he thinks the gentlemen of the country would do very well to make me give some account of myself.

On the other side, some of Sir Roger's friends are afraid the old Knight is imposed upon by a designing fellow, and as they have heard that he converses very promiscuously, when he is in town, do not know but he has brought down with him some discarded Whig, that is sullen and says nothing because he is out of place.

Such is the variety of opinions which are here entertained of me, so that I pass among some for a disaffected person, and among others for a Popish priest; among some for a wizard, and among others for a murderer; and all this for no other reason, that I can imagine, but because I do not hoot and holloa and make a noise. It is true, my friend Sir Roger tells them, *that it is my way*, and that I am only a philosopher; but this will not satisfy them. They think there is more in me than he discovers, and that I do not hold my tongue for nothing.

For these and other reasons I shall set out for London to-morrow, having found by experience that the country is not a place for a person of my temper, who does not love jollity, and what they call good neighborhood. A man that is out of humor when an unexpected guest breaks in upon him, and does not away diseases, and did other beneficent acts ; neither did a little harmless mischief lie wholly out of their way. Dryden says,

> " ' At least as little honest as he could,
> And like white witches mischievously good.' "

W. H. WILLS.

care for sacrificing an afternoon to every chance-
comer, that will be the master of his own time, and
the pursuer of his own inclinations, makes but a very
unsociable figure in this kind of life. I shall therefore retire into the town, if I may make use of that
phrase, and get into the crowd again as fast as I can,
in order to be alone. I can there raise what speculations I please upon others, without being observed
myself, and at the same time enjoy all the advantages
of company with all the privileges of solitude. In
the meanwhile, to finish the month, and conclude
these my rural speculations, I shall here insert a letter from my friend Will Honeycomb, who has not
lived a month for these forty years out of the smoke
of London, and rallies me after his way upon my
country life.

"DEAR SPEC, —
"I suppose this letter will find thee picking of
daisies, or smelling to a lock of hay, or passing away
thy time in some innocent country diversion of the
like nature. I have, however, orders from the club
to summon thee up to town, being all of us cursedly
afraid thou wilt not be able to relish our company,
after thy conversations with Moll White and Will
Wimble. Pr'ythee don't send us up any more stories of a cock and a bull, nor frighten the town with
spirits and witches. Thy speculations begin to smell
confoundedly of woods and meadows. If thou dost
not come up quickly, we shall conclude that thou art
in love with one of Sir Roger's dairy-maids. Service to the Knight. Sir Andrew is grown the cock
of the club since he left us, and if he does not return

quickly will make every mother's son of us Commonwealth's men.

Dear Spec,

Thine eternally,

WILL HONEYCOMB."

XXVI. THE SPECTATOR'S RETURN TO LONDON.

*Qui, aut tempus quid postulet non videt, aut plura loquitur, aut se
ostentat, aut eorum quibuscum est . . . rationem non habet, . . . is inep-
tus esse dicitur.*[1]

CICERO, *De Oratore*, ii. 4; 17.

HAVING notified to my good friend Sir Roger that
I should set out for London the next day, his horses
were ready at the appointed hour in the evening;
and attended by one of his grooms, I arrived at the
county town at twilight, in order to be ready for the
stage-coach the day following. As soon as we arrived at the inn, the servant who waited upon me,
inquired of the chamberlain, in my hearing, what
company he had for the coach. The fellow answered,
"Mrs. Betty Arable, the great fortune, and the
widow her mother; a recruiting officer (who took a
place because they were to go); young Squire Quick-
set, her cousin (that her mother wished her to be
married to); Ephraim,[2] the Quaker, her guardian;
and a gentleman that had studied himself dumb from
Sir Roger de Coverley's." I observed by what he

1. The man who either does not see that he is taking up the
time, or that he talks too much, or makes a display of himself,
or does not take account of the persons he is with, that man is
said to be without tact.

2. Ephraim was a common term for Quakers and was derived
from the description of the man who would not fight, in Psalm
lxviii. 9.

said of myself, that according to his office, he dealt much in intelligence; and doubted not but there was some foundation for his reports of the rest of the company, as well as for the whimsical account he gave of me.

The next morning at daybreak we were all called; and I, who know my own natural shyness, and endeavor to be as little liable to be disputed with as possible, dressed immediately that I might make no one wait. The first preparation for our setting out was, that the captain's half pike was placed near the coachman, and a drum behind the coach. In the mean time the drummer, the captain's equipage, was very loud that none of the captain's things should be placed so as to be spoiled; upon which his cloak bag was fixed in the seat of the coach; and the captain himself, according to a frequent, though invidious behavior of military men, ordered his man to look sharp, that none but one of the ladies should have the place he had taken fronting to the coach-box.

We were in some little time fixed in our seats and sat with that dislike which people not too good-natured usually conceive of each other at first sight. The coach jumbled us insensibly into some sort of familiarity: and we had not moved above two miles, when the widow asked the captain what success he had in his recruiting. The officer, with a frankness he believed very graceful, told her that indeed he had but very little luck, and had suffered much by desertion, therefore should be glad to end his warfare in the service of her or her fair daughter. "In a word," continued he, "I am a soldier, and to be plain is my character: you see me, madam, young, sound, and impudent;[1] take me yourself, widow, or give me to her, I will be wholly at your disposal. I am a soldier of fortune, ha!'' This was followed by a vain laugh of his own, and a deep silence of all the rest of the company. I had nothing left for it but to fall fast asleep, which I did with all speed. "Come," said he, "resolve upon it, we will make a wedding at the next town: we will wake this pleasant companion who has fallen asleep, to be the brideman, and" (giving the Quaker a clap on the knee) he concluded, "this sly saint, who, I 'll warrant, understands what's what as well as you or I, widow, shall give the bride as father."

The Quaker, who happened to be a man of smartness, answered, "Friend, I take it in good part, that thou hast given me the authority of a father over this comely and virtuous child; and I must assure thee, that if I have the giving her, I shall not bestow her on thee. Thy mirth, friend, savoreth of folly: thou art a person of a light mind; thy drum is a type of thee, it soundeth because it is empty. Verily it is not from thy fulness, but thy emptiness, that thou hast spoken this day. Friend, friend, we have hired this coach in partnership with thee to carry us to the great city; we cannot go any other way. This worthy mother must hear thee if thou wilt needs utter thy follies; we cannot help it, friend, I say: if thou wilt, we must hear thee; but if thou wert a man of understanding, thou wouldst not take advantage of thy courageous countenance to abash us children of peace. Thou art, thou sayest, a soldier; give quarter to us, who cannot resist thee. Why didst thou fleer at our friend, who feigned himself asleep? He

1. The captain praises himself for his freedom from bashfulness.

said nothing, but how dost thou know what he con-
taineth? If thou speakest improper things in the
hearing of this virtuous young virgin, consider it is
an outrage against a distressed person that cannot
get from thee: to speak indiscreetly what we are
obliged to hear, by being hasped up with thee in this
public vehicle, is in some degree assaulting on the
high road."

Here Ephraim paused, and the captain with an
happy and uncommon impudence (which can be con-
victed and support itself at the same time) cries,
"Faith, friend, I thank thee; I should have been a
little impertinent if thou hadst not reprimanded me.
Come, thou art, I see, a smoky old fellow, and I 'll
be very orderly the ensuing part of the journey. I
was going to give myself airs, but, ladies, I beg par-
don."

The captain was so little out of humor, and our
company was so far from being soured by this little
ruffle, that Ephraim and he took a particular delight
in being agreeable to each other for the future; and
assumed their different provinces in the conduct of
the company.[1] Our reckonings, apartments, and
accommodation fell under Ephraim; and the captain looked to all disputes on the road, as the good
behavior of our coachman, and the right we had of
taking place as going to London of all vehicles coming from thence.[2]

1. If Steele was describing a journey from Worcester to London, he would have reckoned on three entire days. The coach
did not then travel by night. Fielding's novel of *Joseph Andrews*
gives capital pictures of inns and roads, though the date is a
little later than that of *The Spectator.*
2. "This rule of the road was occasioned by the bad condition

The occurrences we met with were ordinary, and very little happened which could entertain by the relation of them: but when I considered the company we were in, I took it for no small good fortune that the whole journey was not spent in impertinences, which to one part of us might be an entertainment, to the other a suffering.

What, therefore, Ephraim said when we were almost arrived at London, had to me an air not only of good understanding but good breeding. Upon the young lady's expressing her satisfaction in the journey, and declaring how delightful it had been to her, Ephraim declared himself as follows: "There is no ordinary part of human life which expresseth so much a good mind, and a right inward man, as his behavior upon meeting with strangers, especially such as may seem the most unsuitable companions to him: such a man, when he falleth in the way with persons of simplicity and innocence, however knowing he may be in the ways of men, will not vaunt himself thereof; but will the rather hide his superiority to them, that he may not be painful unto them. My good friend " (continued he, turning to the officer), "thee and I are to part by and by, and peradventure we may never meet again: but be advised by a plain man: modes and apparel are but trifles to the real man, therefore do not think such a man as thyself terrible for thy garb, nor such a one as me con-

of the public ways. On the best lines of communication ruts were so deep and obstructions so formidable that it was only in fine weather that the whole breadth of the road was available; for on each side was often a quagmire of mud. Seldom could two vehicles pass each other unless one of them stopped."—
W. H. WILLS.

temptible for mine. When two such as thee and I meet, with affections as we ought to have towards each other, thou shouldst rejoice to see my peaceable demeanor, and I should be glad to see thy strength and ability to protect me in it."

XXVII. SIR ROGER AND SIR ANDREW.

Hæc memini et victum frustra contendere Thyrsin.[1]
VIRGIL, *Eclogues*, vii. 69.

THERE is scarce anything more common than animosities between parties that cannot subsist but by their agreement: this was well represented in the sedition of the members of the human body in the old Roman fable.[2] It is often the case of lesser confederate states against a superior power, which are hardly held together, though their unanimity is necessary for their common safety; and this is always the case of the landed and trading interests of Great Britain; the trader is fed by the product of the land, and the landed man cannot be clothed but by the skill of the trader: and yet those interests are ever jarring.

We had last winter an instance of this at our club, in Sir Roger de Coverley and Sir Andrew Freeport, between whom there is generally a constant, though friendly opposition of opinions. It happened that one of the company, in an historical discourse, was observing, that Carthaginian faith was a proverbial phrase to intimate breach of leagues. Sir Roger said

1. I call to mind these things, and especially how Thyrsis, when put down, kept on arguing.
2. A notable use of this story, first recorded by Livy, is in Shakespeare's *Coriolanus*, act I., scene 1.

it could hardly be otherwise: that the Carthaginians were the greatest traders in the world; and as gain is the chief end of such a people, they never pursue any other: the means to it are never regarded; they will, if it comes easily, get money honestly; but if not, they will not scruple to attain it by fraud, or cozenage: and indeed, what is the whole business of the trader's account, but to overreach him who trusts to his memory? But were that not so, what can there great and noble be expected from him whose attention is forever fixed upon balancing his books, and watching over his expenses? And at best let frugality and parsimony be the virtues of the merchant, how much is his punctual dealing below a gentleman's charity to the poor, or hospitality among his neighbors?

Captain Sentry observed Sir Andrew very diligent in hearing Sir Roger, and had a mind to turn the discourse, by taking notice in general, from the highest to the lowest parts of human society, there was a secret, though unjust, way among men, of indulging the seeds of ill-nature and envy, by comparing their own state of life to that of another, and grudging the approach of their neighbor to their own happiness; and on the other side, he, who is the less at his ease, repines at the other, who he thinks has unjustly the advantage over him. Thus the civil and military lists look upon each other with much ill-nature; the soldier repines at the courtier's power, and the courtier rallies the soldier's honor; or, to come to lower instances, the private men in the horse and foot of an army, the carmen and coachmen in the city streets, mutually look upon each other with ill-will, when they are in competition for quarters, or the way in their respective motions.

"It is very well, good captain," interrupted Sir Andrew: " you may attempt to turn the discourse if you think fit; but I must however have a word or two with Sir Roger, who, I see, thinks he has paid me off, and been very severe upon the merchant. I shall not," continued he, " at this time remind Sir Roger of the great and noble monuments of charity and public spirit, which have been erected by merchants since the reformation, but at present content myself with what he allows us, parsimony and frugality. If it were consistent with the quality of so ancient a baronet as Sir Roger, to keep an account, or measure things by the most infallible way, that of numbers, he would prefer our parsimony to his hospitality. If to drink so many hogsheads is to be hospitable, we do not contend for the fame of that virtue; but it would be worth while to consider, whether so many artificers at work ten days together by my appointment, or so many peasants made merry on Sir Roger's charge, are the men more obliged? I believe the families of the artificers will thank me more than the households of the peasants shall Sir Roger. Sir Roger gives to his men, but I place mine above the necessity or obligation of my bounty. I am in very little pain for the Roman proverb upon the Carthaginian traders; the Romans were their professed enemies: I am only sorry no Carthaginian histories have come to our hands: we might have been taught perhaps by them some proverbs against the Roman generosity, in fighting for, and bestowing other people's goods. But since Sir Roger has taken occasion, from an old proverb, to be out of humor with merchants, it should be no offence to offer one not quite so old, in their defence. When a man

happens to break in Holland, they say of him that
' he has not kept true accounts.' This phrase, perhaps, among us, would appear a soft or humorous
way of speaking, but with that exact nation it bears
the highest reproach. For a man to be mistaken in
the calculation of his expense, in his ability to answer
future demands, or to be impertinently sanguine in
putting his credit to too great adventure, are all instances of as much infamy, as with gayer nations
to be failing in courage, or common honesty.

"Numbers are so much the measure of everything
that is valuable, that it is not possible to demonstrate
the success of any action, or the prudence of any undertaking, without them. I say this in answer to
what Sir Roger is pleased to say, ' that little that is
truly noble can be expected from one who is ever
poring on his cash-book, or balancing his accounts.'
When I have my returns from abroad, I can tell to
a shilling, by the help of numbers, the profit or loss
by my adventure; but I ought also to be able to show
that I had reason for making it, either from my own
experience or that of other people, or from a reasonable presumption that my returns will be sufficient
to answer my expense and hazard; and this is never
to be done without the skill of numbers. For instance, if I am to trade to Turkey, I ought beforehand to know the demand of our manufactures there,
as well as of their silks in England, and the customary prices that are given for both in each country.
I ought to have a clear knowledge of these matters
beforehand, that I may presume upon sufficient returns to answer the charge of the cargo I have fitted
out, the freight and assurance out and home, the customs to the queen, and the interest of my own money,

and besides all these expenses a reasonable profit to myself. Now what is there of scandal in this skill? What has the merchant done, that he should be so little in the good graces of Sir Roger? He throws down no man's enclosures, and tramples upon no man's corn; he takes nothing from the industrious laborer; he pays the poor man for his work; he communicates his profit with mankind; by the preparation of his cargo, and the manufacture of his returns, he furnishes employment and subsistence to greater numbers than the richest nobleman; and even the nobleman is obliged to him for finding out foreign markets for the produce of his estate, and for making a great addition to his rents: and yet 't is certain that none of all these things could be done by him without the exercise of his skill in numbers.

"This is the economy of the merchant, and the conduct of the gentleman must be the same, unless by scorning to be the steward, he resolves the steward shall be the gentleman. The gentleman, no more than the merchant, is able, without the help of numbers, to account for the success of any action, or the prudence of any adventure. If, for instance, the chase is his whole adventure, his only returns must be the stag's horns in the great hall, and the fox's nose upon the stable door. Without doubt Sir Roger knows the full value of these returns: and if beforehand he had computed the charges of the chase, a gentleman of his discretion would certainly have hanged up all his dogs: he would never have brought back so many fine horses to the kennel; he would never have gone so often, like a blast, over fields of corn. If such too had been the conduct of all his ancestors, he might truly have boasted at this

day, that the antiquity of his family had never been
sullied by a trade; a merchant had never been permitted with his whole estate to purchase a room for
his picture in the gallery of the Coverleys, or to
claim his descent from the maid of honor. But 't is
very happy for Sir Roger that the merchant paid so
dear for his ambition. 'T is the misfortune of many
other gentlemen to turn out of the seats of their ancestors, to make way for such new masters as have
been more exact in their accounts than themselves;
and certainly he deserves the estate a great deal better who has got it by his industry, than he who has
lost it by his negligence."

XXVIII. THE CRIES OF LONDON.

. . . Linguæ centum sunt, oraque centum,
Ferrea vox.[1] *. . .*

VIRGIL, *Æneid*, vi. 625.

THERE is nothing which more astonishes a for-
eigner, and frights a country squire, than the Cries
of London. My good friend Sir Roger often de-
clares, that he cannot get them out of his head, or
go to sleep for them, the first week that he is in
town. On the contrary, Will Honeycomb calls them
the *Ramage de la Ville*,[2] and prefers them to the
sounds of larks and nightingales, with all the music of
the fields and woods. I have lately received a letter
from some very odd fellow upon this subject, which I
shall leave with my reader, without saying anything
further of it.

1. A hundred mouths, a hundred tongues,
     And throats of brass, inspir'd with iron lungs. — DRYDEN
2. Town warblers.

"Sir, —

"I am a man of all business, and would willingly turn my head to anything for an honest livelihood. I have invented several projects for raising many millions of money without burthening the subject, but I cannot get the parliament to listen to me, who look upon me, forsooth, as a crack[1] and a projector; so that despairing to enrich either myself or my country by this public-spiritedness, I would make some proposals to you relating to a design which I have very much at heart, and which may procure me a handsome subsistence, if you will be pleased to recommend it to the cities of London and Westminster.

"The post I would aim at is to be Comptroller-general of the London Cries, which are at present under no manner of rules or discipline. I think I am pretty well qualified for this place, as being a man of very strong lungs, of great insight into all the branches of our British trades and manufactures, and of a competent skill in music.

"The cries of London may be divided into vocal and instrumental. As for the latter, they are at present under a very great disorder. A freeman[2] of London has the privilege of disturbing a whole street for an hour together, with the twanking of a brass kettle or a frying-pan. The watchman's thump at midnight startles us in our beds, as much as the breaking in of a thief. The sowgelder's horn has indeed something musical in it, but this is seldom

1. If Addison had been writing to-day he would probably have used the word " crank."
2. A member that is of one of the corporations, which were given certain privileges.

heard within the liberties. I would therefore propose, that no instrument of this nature should be
made use of, which I have not tuned and licensed,
after having carefully examined in what manner it
may affect the ears of her Majesty's liege subjects.

"Vocal cries are of a much larger extent, and,
indeed, so full of incongruities and barbarisms, that
we appear a distracted city to foreigners, who do not
comprehend the meaning of such enormous outcries.
Milk is generally sold in a note above *ela,*[1] and in
sounds so exceeding shrill, that it often sets our teeth
on edge. The chimney-sweeper is confined to no
certain pitch; he sometimes utters himself in the
deepest base, and sometimes in the sharpest treble;
sometimes in the highest, and sometimes in the lowest note of the gamut. The same observation might
be made on the retailers of small coal, not to mention
broken glasses or brick-dust. In these, therefore,
and the like cases, it should be my care to sweeten
and mellow the voices of these itinerant tradesmen,
before they make their appearance in our streets, as
also to accommodate their cries to their respective
wares; and to take care in particular that those may
not make the most noise who have the least to sell,
which is very observable in the venders of card-
matches, to whom I cannot but apply that old proverb of 'Much cry, but little wool.'

"Some of these last mentioned musicians are so
very loud in the sale of these trifling manufactures,
that an honest splenetic gentleman of my acquaintance bargained with one of them never to come into
the street where he lived: but what was the effect of
this contract? why, the whole tribe of card-match·

1. That is, a note above *la* or A.

makers which frequent that quarter, passed by his
door the very next day, in hopes of being bought off
after the same manner.

"It is another great imperfection in our London
cries, that there is no just time nor measure observed
in them. Our news should, indeed, be published in
a very quick time, because it is a commodity that
will not keep cold. It should not, however, be cried
with the same precipitation as 'fire:' yet this is generally the case. A bloody battle alarms the town
from one end to another in an instant. Every motion of the French is published in so great a hurry,
that one would think the enemy were at our gates.
This likewise I would take upon me to regulate in
such a manner, that there should be some distinction
made between the spreading of a victory, a march,
or an encampment, a Dutch, a Portugal, or a Spanish mail. Nor must I omit, under this head, those
excessive alarms with which several boisterous rustics
infest our streets in turnip season; and which are
more inexcusable, because these are wares which are
in no danger of cooling upon their hands.

"There are others who affect a very slow time,
and are, in my opinion, much more tunable than the
former; the cooper, in particular, swells his last note
in an hollow voice, that is not without its harmony:
nor can I forbear being inspired with a most agreeable melancholy, when I hear that sad and solemn
air with which the public are very often asked, if they
have any chairs to mend? Your own memory may
suggest to you many other lamentable ditties of the
same nature, in which the music is wonderfully lan-
guishing and melodious.

"I am always pleased with that particular time of

the year which is proper for the pickling of dill and cucumbers; but, alas, this cry, like the song of the nightingale, is not heard above two months. It would, therefore, be worth while, to consider whether the same air might not in some cases be adapted to other words.

"It might likewise deserve our most serious consideration, how far, in a well-regulated city, those humorists are to be tolerated, who, not contented with the traditional cries of their forefathers, have invented particular songs, and tunes of their own: such as was, not many years since, the pastry-man, commonly known by the name of the colly-molly-puff; and such as is at this day the vender of powder and wash-balls, who, if I am rightly informed, goes under the name of Powder Watt.

"I must not here omit one particular absurdity which runs through this whole vociferous generation, and which renders their cries very often not only incommodious, but altogether useless to the public; I mean that idle accomplishment which they all of them aim at, of crying so as not to be understood. Whether or no they have learned this from several of our affected singers, I will not take upon me to say; but most certain it is, that people know the wares they deal in rather by their tunes than by their words; insomuch, that I have sometimes seen a country boy run out to buy apples of a bellows-mender, and ginger-bread from a grinder of knives and scissors. Nay, so strangely infatuated are some very eminent artists of this particular grace in a cry, that none but their acquaintance are able to guess at their profession; for who else can know that 'Work if I had it' should be the signification of a corn-cutter.

"Forasmuch, therefore, as persons of this rank are seldom men of genius or capacity, I think it would be very proper, that some man of good sense, and sound judgment, should preside over these public cries, who should permit none to lift up their voices in our streets, that have not tuneable throats, and are not only able to overcome the noise of the crowd, and the rattling of coaches, but also to vend their respective merchandises in apt phrases, and in the most distinct and agreeable sounds. I do therefore humbly recommend myself as a person rightly qualified for this post: and if I meet with fitting encouragement, shall communicate some other projects which I have by me, that may no less conduce to the emolument of the public.

" I am, Sir, &c.

"RALPH CROTCHET."

XXIX. SIR ROGER COMES TO TOWN.

> *Ævo rarissima nostro*
> *Simplicitas.*[1]
>
> OVID, *Ars Amatoria,* i. 241.

I WAS this morning surprised with a great knocking at the door, when my landlady's daughter came up to me, and told me that there was a man below desired to speak with me. Upon my asking her who it was, she told me it was a very grave elderly person, but that she did not know his name. I immediately went down to him, and found him to be the coachman of my worthy friend Sir Roger de Coverley. He told me that his master came to town last night, and would be glad to take a turn with me in

1. Most rare is now our old simplicity. — DRYDEN.

Gray's Inn Walks. As I was wondering in myself what had brought Sir Roger to town, not having lately received any letter from him, he told me that his master was come up to get a sight of Prince Eugene,[1] and that he desired I would immediately meet him.

I was not a little pleased with the curiosity of the old Knight, though I did not much wonder at it, having heard him say more than once in private discourse, that he looked upon Prince Eugenio (for so the Knight always calls him) to be a greater man than Scanderbeg.[2]

I was no sooner come into Gray's Inn Walks, but I heard my friend upon the terrace hemming twice or thrice to himself with great vigor, for he loves to clear his pipes in good air (to make use of his own phrase), and is not a little pleased with any one who takes notice of the strength which he still exerts in his morning hems.

I was touched with a secret joy at the sight of the good old man, who before he saw me was engaged in conversation with a beggar-man that had asked an alms of him. I could hear my friend chide him for not finding out some work; but at the same time saw

1. Prince Eugene of Savoy (1667–1736) shared with the Duke of Marlborough in the honors which fell to the English, Austrian, and Dutch forces in the war with France and Spain which was now drawing to a close. In the intrigues of English politics the enemies of Marlborough endeavored to make a breach between him and Eugene, but without success. The enthusiasm over the prince was very great, so that the houses and streets were crowded whenever he went abroad.

2. Iskander (Alexander) Bey, the name by which the heroic George Castriot, an Albanian who fought the Turks in the latter half of the fifteenth century, was known.

him put his hand in his pocket and give him six-
pence.

Our salutations were very hearty on both sides,
consisting of many kind shakes of the hand, and several affectionate looks which we cast upon one another. After which the Knight told me my good
friend his chaplain was very well, and much at my
service, and that the Sunday before he had made a
most incomparable sermon out of Doctor Barrow.
"I have left," says he, "all my affairs in his hands,
and being willing to lay an obligation upon him,
have deposited with him thirty marks,[1] to be distributed among his poor parishioners."

He then proceeded to acquaint me with the welfare
of Will Wimble. Upon which he put his hand into
his fob and presented me in his name with a tobacco-
stopper, telling me that Will had been busy all the
beginning of the winter, in turning great quantities
of them; and that he made a present of one to every
gentleman in the country who has good principles,
and smokes. He added, that poor Will was at present under great tribulation, for that Tom Touchy
had taken the law of him for cutting some hazel
sticks out of one of his hedges.

Among other pieces of news which the Knight
brought from his country seat, he informed me that
Moll White was dead; and that about a month after
her death the wind was so very high, that it blew
down the end of one of his barns. "But for my
own part," says Sir Roger, "I do not think that the
old woman had any hand in it."

He afterwards fell into an account of the diver-

1. The value of a mark, which was not, however, a coin any
more than a guinea is, was thirteen shillings and fourpence.

sions which had passed in his house during the holidays; for Sir Roger, after the laudable custom of his ancestors, always keeps open house at Christmas. I learned from him that he had killed eight fat hogs for the season, that he had dealt about his chines very liberally amongst his neighbors, and that in particular he had sent a string of hogs-puddings with a pack of cards to every poor family in the parish. "I have often thought," says Sir Roger, "it happens very well that Christmas should fall out in the middle of the winter. It is the most dead uncomfortable time of the year, when the poor people would suffer very much from their poverty and cold, if they had not good cheer, warm fires, and Christmas gambols to support them. I love to rejoice their poor hearts at this season, and to see the whole village merry in my great hall. I allow a double quantity of malt to my small beer, and set it a running for twelve days to every one that calls for it. I have always a piece of cold beef and a mince-pie upon the table, and am wonderfully pleased to see my tenants pass away a whole evening in playing their innocent tricks, and smutting one another. Our friend Will Wimble is as merry as any of them, and shows a thousand roguish tricks upon these occasions."

I was very much delighted with the reflection of my old friend, which carried so much goodness in it. He then launched out into the praise of the late Act of Parliament [1] for securing the Church of England, and told me, with great satisfaction, that he believed it already began to take effect, for that a rigid Dis-

1. An act designed to strengthen the Test Act, which required all persons holding offices under the crown to take the Sacrament according to the rites of the Church of England.

senter, who chanced to dine at his house on Christmas day, had been observed to eat very plentifully of his plum-porridge.

After having dispatched all our country matters, Sir Roger made several inquiries concerning the club, and particularly of his old antagonist Sir Andrew Freeport. He asked me with a kind of smile whether Sir Andrew had not taken advantage of his absence to vent among them some of his republican doctrines; but soon after, gathering up his countenance into a more than ordinary seriousness, "Tell me truly," says he, "don't you think Sir Andrew had a hand in the Pope's Procession?"[1] — but without giving me time to answer him, "Well, well," says he, "I know you are a wary man, and do not care to talk of public matters."

The Knight then asked me if I had seen Prince Eugenio, and made me promise to get him a stand[2] in some convenient place where he might have a full sight of that extraordinary man, whose presence does so much honor to the British nation. He dwelt very long on the praises of this great general, and I found that, since I was with him in the country, he had drawn many observations together out of his reading in Baker's Chronicle,[3] and other authors, who always

1. The 17th of November, the date of Queen Elizabeth's accession, was still celebrated by carrying in procession the head of the Pope in effigy, which was afterward burned. At the anniversary just passed party feeling ran high in consequence of the treaty impending with France, which was looked upon as a concession to the papal interests, and the authorities seized these effigies.

2. The prince Eugenio stood godfather to a child of Steele, so *The Spectator* might be expected to have some influence.

3. *Chronicle of the Kings of England from the time of the*

lie in his hall window, which very much redound to the honor of this prince.

Having passed away the greatest part of the morning in hearing the Knight's reflections, which were partly private, and partly political, he asked me if I would smoke a pipe with him over a dish of coffee at Squire's. As I love the old man, I take delight in complying with everything that is agreeable to him, and accordingly waited on him to the coffee-house, where his venerable figure drew upon us the eyes of the whole room. He had no sooner seated himself at the upper end of the high table, but he called for a clean pipe, a paper of tobacco, a dish of coffee, a wax candle, and the Supplement,[1] with such an air of cheerfulness and good-humor, that all the boys in the coffee-room (who seemed to take pleasure in serving him) were at once employed on his several errands, insomuch that nobody else could come at a dish of tea, till the Knight had got all his conveniences about him.

XXX. SIR ROGER IN WESTMINSTER ABBEY.

Ire tamen restat, Numa quò devenit, et Ancus.[2]
HORACE, *Epistles*, I. v. 27.

MY friend Sir Roger de Coverley told me t'other night that he had been reading my paper upon West-

Romans' Government unto the Death of King James, by Sir Richard Baker.

1. Publishers of newspapers then issued supplements at later hours than the regular edition, when special news came in.

2. Still it remains to go whither Numa has gone down, and Ancus.

minster Abbey,[1] in which, says he, there are a great many ingenious fancies. He told me, at the same time, that he observed I had promised another paper upon the tombs, and that he should be glad to go and see them with me, not having visited them since he had read history. I could not at first imagine how this came into the Knight's head, till I recollected that he had been very busy all last summer upon Baker's Chronicle, which he has quoted several times in his disputes with Sir Andrew Freeport since his last coming to town. Accordingly, I promised to call upon him the next morning, that we might go together to the Abbey.

I found the Knight under his butler's hands, who always shaves him. He was no sooner dressed than he called for a glass of the Widow Trueby's water,[2] which he told me he always drank before he went abroad. He recommended me to a dram of it at the same time with so much heartiness, that I could not forbear drinking it. As soon as I had got it down, I found it very unpalatable; upon which the Knight, observing that I had made several wry faces, told me that he knew I should not like it at first, but that it was the best thing in the world against the stone or gravel.

I could have wished, indeed, that he had acquainted me with the virtues of it sooner; but it was too late to complain, and I knew what he had done was out of good-will. Sir Roger told me, further, that he looked upon it to be very good for a man whilst he

1. Addison's paper is No. 26, published March 30, the previous year.

2. It was a time of innumerable compounds supposed to act as tonics or curatives. Brandy was the base of most of them.

stayed in town, to keep off infection; and that he got together a quantity of it upon the first news of the sickness being at Dantzic.[1] When of a sudden, turning short to one of his servants, who stood behind him, he bade him call a hackney-coach, and take care it was an elderly man that drove it.

He then resumed his discourse upon Mrs. Trueby's water, telling me that the Widow Trueby was one who did more good than all the doctors and apothecaries in the county; that she distilled every poppy that grew within five miles of her; that she distributed her water gratis among all sorts of people: to which the Knight added, that she had a very great jointure, and that the whole country would fain have it a match between him and her; "And truly," says Sir Roger, "if I had not been engaged,[2] perhaps I could not have done better."

His discourse was broken off by his man's telling him he had called a coach. Upon our going to it, after having cast his eye upon the wheels, he asked the coachman if his axletree was good; upon the fellow's telling him he would warrant it, the Knight turned to me, told me he looked like an honest man, and went in without further ceremony.

We had not gone far, when Sir Roger, popping out his head, called the coachman down from his box, and, upon his presenting himself at the window, asked him if he smoked: as I was considering what this would end in, he bade him stop by the way at any good tobacconist's, and take in a roll of their

1. The great plague of Dantzic which swept away nearly half the inhabitants was in 1709.

2. Not in the sense of betrothed, but in that of having his affections engaged.

best Virginia. Nothing material happened in the remaining part of our journey till we were set down at the west end of the Abbey.

As we went up the body of the church, the Knight pointed at the trophies upon one of the new monu ments, and cried out, "A brave man, I warrant him!" Passing afterwards by Sir Cloudesley Shovel,[1] he flung his hand that way, and cried, "Sir Cloudesley Shovel! a very gallant 'man!" As we stood before Busby's[2] tomb, the Knight uttered himself again after the same manner, — "Dr. Busby — a great man! he whipped my grandfather — a very great man! I should have gone to him myself if I had not been a blockhead — a very great man!"

We were immediately conducted into the little chapel[3] on the right hand. Sir Roger, planting himself at our historian's elbow, was very attentive to everything he said, particularly to the account he gave us of the lord who had cut off the King of Morocco's head. Among several other figures, he was very well pleased to see the statesman Cecil[4] upon his knees; and, concluding them all to be great men, was conducted to the figure which represents that martyr to good housewifery, who died by the prick of a needle.[5] Upon our interpreter's telling us

1. An English admiral who was drowned in 1707 when his fleet was wrecked off the Scilly Isles.

2. Dr. Busby was headmaster of Westminster school for fifty-five years. Although he died in 1695, a game of cards known as Dr. Busby's school was familiar in America a generation ago, and perhaps has not yet gone wholly out of play.

3. The chapel of St. Edmund.

4. The great Lord Burleigh of Elizabeth's reign.

5. Addison is probably slyly repeating the verger's foolish tale. The figure is of Elizabeth Russell, who is pointing her forefinger at a death's skull on the pedestal.

that she was a maid of honor to Queen Elizabeth, the Knight was very inquisitive into her name and family; and, after having regarded her finger for some time, "I wonder," says he, "that Sir Richard Baker has said nothing of her in his Chronicle."

We were then conveyed to the two coronation chairs, where my old friend, after having heard that the stone underneath the most ancient of them, which was brought from Scotland, was called Jacob's Pillar,[1] sat himself down in the chair; and, looking like the figure of an old Gothic king, asked our interpreter what authority they had to say that Jacob had ever been in Scotland. The fellow, instead of returning him an answer, told him that he hoped his honor would pay his forfeit. I could observe Sir Roger a little ruffled upon being thus trepanned; but, our guide not insisting upon his demand, the Knight soon recovered his good humor, and whispered in my ear that if Will Wimble were with us, and saw those two chairs, it would go hard but he would get a tobacco-stopper out of one or t'other of them.

Sir Roger, in the next place, laid his hand upon Edward the Third's sword, and, leaning upon the pommel of it, gave us the whole history of the Black Prince; concluding that, in Sir Richard Baker's opinion, Edward the Third was one of the greatest princes that ever sat upon the English throne.

We were then shown Edward the Confessor's tomb, upon which Sir Roger acquainted us that he

1. Jacob's Pillar or pillow was the name given to the stone which was set in the chair in which Scottish kings had been crowned since the ninth century till Edward the First brought it to Westminster in 1297 upon the conquest of Scotland.

was the first who touched for the evil,[1] and afterwards Henry the Fourth's, upon which he shook his
head, and told us there was fine reading in the cas-
ualties in that reign.

Our conductor then pointed to that monument
where there is the figure of one of our English kings
without an head;[2] and upon giving us to know that
the head, which was of beaten silver, had been stolen
away several years since, "Some Whig, I 'll warrant
you," says Sir Roger: "you ought to lock up your
kings better; they will carry off the body too if you
don't take care."

The glorious names of Henry the Fifth and Queen
Elizabeth gave the Knight great opportunities of
shining and of doing justice to Sir Richard Baker,
who, as our Knight observed with some surprise, had
a great many kings in him whose monuments he had
not seen in the Abbey.

For my own part, I could not but be pleased to
see the Knight show such an honest passion for the
glory of his country, and such a respectful gratitude
to the memory of its princes.

I must not omit that the benevolence of my good
old friend, which flows out towards every one he converses with, made him very kind to our interpreter,
whom he looked upon as an extraordinary man; for
which reason he shook him by the hand at parting,

1. Scrofula was called the "king's evil" from the superstition
that it could be cured by the touch of a king truly anointed.
The superstition was by no means dead in Queen Anne's time.
Dr. Johnson, who was a victim of the disease, remembered being
taken to Queen Anne to be cured.

2. The king without a head was Henry V. The head had been
of solid silver, the rest of the figure being plated.

telling him that he should be very glad to see him at his lodgings in Norfolk Buildings, and talk over these matters with him more at leisure.

XXXI. SIR ROGER UPON BEARDS.

Stolidam præbet tibi vellere barbam.[1]

PERSIUS, *Satires*, ii. 28.

WHEN I was last with my friend Sir Roger in Westminster Abbey, I observed that he stood longer than ordinary before the bust of a venerable old man. I was at a loss to guess the reason of it; when, after some time, he pointed to the figure, and asked me if I did not think that our forefathers looked much wiser in their beards than we do without them? "For my part," says he, "when I am walking in my gallery in the country, and see my ancestors, who many of them died before they were of my age, I cannot forbear regarding them as so many old patriarchs, and at the same time looking upon myself as an idle smockfaced young fellow. I love to see your Abrahams, your Isaacs, and your Jacobs, as we have them in old pieces of tapestry, with beards below their girdles, that cover half the hangings." The Knight added, "if I would recommend beards in one of my papers, and endeavor to restore human faces to their ancient dignity, that, upon a month's warning he would undertake to lead up the fashion himself in a pair of whiskers."

I smiled at my friend's fancy; but, after we parted, could not forbear reflecting on the metamor-phosis our faces have undergone in this particular.

The beard, conformable to the notion of my friend

1. "Holds out his foolish beard for thee to pluck."

Sir Roger, was for many ages looked upon as the type of wisdom. Lucian more than once rallies the philosophers of his time, who endeavored to rival one another in beard; and represents a learned man who stood for a professorship in philosophy, as unqualified for it by the shortness of his beard.

Ælian, in his account of Zoilus, the pretended critic, who wrote against Homer and Plato, and thought himself wiser than all who had gone before him, tells us that this Zoilus had a very long beard that hung down upon his breast, but no hair upon his head, which he always kept close shaved, regarding, it seems, the hairs of his head as so many suckers, which, if they had been suffered to grow, might have drawn away the nourishment from his chin, and by that means have starved his beard.

I have read somewhere, that one of the popes refused to accept an edition of a saint's works, which were presented to him, because the saint, in his effigies before the book, was drawn without a beard.

We see by these instances what homage the world has formerly paid to beards; and that a barber was not then allowed to make those depredations on the faces of the learned, which have been permitted him of later years.

Accordingly several wise nations have been so extremely jealous of the least ruffle offered to their beard, that they seem to have fixed the point of honor principally in that part. The Spaniards were wonderfully tender in this particular. Don Quevedo, in his third vision on the last judgment, has carried the humor very far, when he tells us that one of his vain-glorious countrymen, after having received sentence, was taken into custody by a couple of evil spirits; but that his guides happening to disorder his mustachoes, they were forced to recompose them with a pair of curling-irons, before they could get him to file off.

If we look into the history of our own nation, we shall find that the beard flourished in the Saxon heptarchy, but was very much discouraged under the Norman line. It shot out, however, from time to time, in several reigns under different shapes. The last effort it made seems to have been in Queen Mary's days, as the curious reader may find if he pleases to peruse the figures of Cardinal Pole and Bishop Gardiner; though, at the same time, I think it may be questioned, if zeal against popery has not induced our Protestant painters to extend the beards of these two persecutors beyond their natural dimensions, in order to make them appear the more terrible.

I find but few beards worth taking notice of in the reign of King James the First.

During the civil wars there appeared one, which makes too great a figure in story to be passed over in silence: I mean that of the redoubted Hudibras,[1] an account of which Butler has transmitted to posterity in the following lines:

> His tawny beard was th' equal grace
> Both of his wisdom and his face;
> In cut and dye so like a tile,
> A sudden view it would beguile;
> The upper part thereof was whey,
> The nether orange mixt with gray.

The whisker continued for some time among us after the expiration of beards; but this is a subject

1. A famous satire on the Puritans by Samuel Butler, published in three parts in 1663, 1664, 1678.

which I shall not here enter upon, having discussed it at large in a distinct treatise, which I keep by me in manuscript, upon the mustachoe.

If my friend Sir Roger's project of introducing beards should take effect, I fear the luxury of the present age would make it a very expensive fashion. There is no question but the beaux would soon provide themselves with false ones of the lightest colors and the most immoderate lengths. A fair beard, of the tapestry size Sir Roger seems to approve, could not come under twenty guineas. The famous golden beard of Æsculapius would hardly be more valuable than one made in the extravagance of the fashion.

Besides, we are not certain that the ladies would not come into the mode, when they take the air on horseback. They already appear in hats and feathers, coats and periwigs; and I see no reason why we should not suppose that they would have their riding-beards on the same occasion.

XXXII. SIR ROGER AT THE PLAY.

Respicere exemplar vitæ morumque jubebo
Doctum imitatorem, et veras hinc ducere voces.[1]
HORACE, *Ars Poetica*, 327, 328.

MY friend Sir Roger de Coverley, when we last met together at the Club, told me that he had a great mind to see the new tragedy [2] with me, assuring me,

1. I 'll bid him look for a model of life and manners,
   Make him a skilled copyist : so shall he shape his speech aright.

2. Addison was ready to use his creation in the way of helping his friend Ambrose Phillips who had translated and adapted to the English stage Racine's *Andromaque* under the title *The Distressed Mother.*

at the same time, that he had not been at a play these twenty years. "The last I saw," said Sir Roger, "was the 'Committee,'[1] which I should not have gone to neither, had not I been told beforehand that it was a good Church of England comedy." He then proceeded to inquire of me who this distressed mother was, and, upon hearing that she was Hector's widow, he told me that her husband was a brave man, and that when he was a school-boy, he had read his life at the end of the dictionary. My friend asked me, in the next place, if there would not be some danger in coming home late, in case the Mohocks[2] should be abroad. "I assure you," says he, "I thought I had fallen into their hands last night, for I observed two or three lusty black men that followed me half way up Fleet Street, and mended their pace behind me in proportion as I put on to get away from them. You must know," continued the Knight with a smile, "I fancied they had a mind to *hunt* me, for I remember an honest gentleman in my neighborhood who was served such a trick in King Charles the Second's time; for which reason he has not ventured himself in town ever since. I might have shown them very good sport had this been their design; for, as I am an old foxhunter, I should have turned and

1. *The Committee, or The Faithful Irishman,* by Sir Robert Howard, Dryden's brother-in-law, was a play ridiculing the Puritans, which was put on the stage in the early days of the Restoration.

2. A gang of London rowdies who infested the streets at this time. They are frequently referred to in *The Spectator,* and their name is one of the forms of Mohawk. It will be remembered that Queen Anne's war was at its height at this time, and many stories were current in London of the ferocity of the Mohawk Indians.

dodged, and have played them a thousand tricks they had never seen in their lives before." Sir Roger added that if these gentlemen had any such intention they did not succeed very well in it; "for I threw them out," says he, "at the end of Norfolk Street, where I doubled the corner and got shelter in my lodgings before they could imagine what was become of me. However," says the Knight, "if Captain Sentry will make one with us to-morrow night, and if you will both of you call upon me about four o'clock, that we may be at the house before it is full, I will have my own coach in readiness to attend you, for John tells me he has got the fore wheels mended."

The captain, who did not fail to meet me there at the appointed hour, bid Sir Roger fear nothing, for that he had put on the same sword which he made use of at the battle of Steenkirk. Sir Roger's servants, and among the rest my old friend the butler, had, I found, provided themselves with good oaken plants to attend their master upon this occasion. When he had placed him in his coach, with myself at his left hand, the captain before him, and his butler at the head of his footmen in the rear, we convoyed him in safety to the playhouse, where, after having marched up the entry in good order, the captain and I went in with him, and seated him betwixt us in the pit. As soon as the house was full, and the candles lighted, my old friend stood up and looked about him with that pleasure which a mind seasoned with humanity naturally feels in itself at the sight of a multitude of people who seem pleased with one another, and partake of the same common entertainment. I could not but fancy to myself, as the old man stood up in the middle of the pit, that

he made a very proper centre to a tragic audience.
Upon the entering of Pyrrhus, the Knight told me
that he did not believe the King of France himself
had a better strut. I was, indeed, very attentive to
my old friend's remarks, because I looked upon them
as a piece of natural criticism; and was well pleased
to hear him, at the conclusion of almost every scene,
telling me that he could not imagine how the play
would end. One while he appeared much concerned
for Andromache; and a little while after as much for
Hermione; and was extremely puzzled to think what
would become of Pyrrhus.

When Sir Roger saw Andromache's obstinate re-
fusal to her lover's importunities, he whispered me
in the ear, that he was sure she would never have
him; to which he added, with a more than ordinary
vehemence, "You can't imagine, Sir, what 't is to
have to do with a widow." Upon Pyrrhus his threat-
ening afterwards to leave her, the Knight shook his
head, and muttered to himself, "Ay, do if you can."
This part dwelt so much upon my friend's imagination, that at the close of the third act, as I was
thinking of something else, he whispered in my ear,
"These widows, Sir, are the most perverse creatures
in the world. But pray," says he, "you that are a
critic, is this play according to your dramatic rules,
as you call them? Should your people in tragedy
always talk to be understood? Why, there is not a
single sentence in this play that I do not know the
meaning of."

The fourth act very luckily begun before I had
time to give the old gentleman an answer: "Well,"
says the Knight, sitting down with great satisfaction,
"I suppose we are now to see Hector's ghost." He

then renewed his attention, and, from time to time,
fell a praising the widow. He made, indeed, a little
mistake as to one of her pages, whom at his first entering he took for Astyanax; but he quickly set himself
right in that particular, though, at the same time, he
owned he should have been very glad to have seen
the little boy, "who," says he, "must needs be a
very fine child by the account that is given of him."
Upon Hermione's going off with a menace to
Pyrrhus, the audience gave a loud clap, to which Sir
Roger added, "On my word, a notable young baggage!"

As there was a very remarkable silence and still-
ness in the audience during the whole action, it was
natural for them to take the opportunity of these
intervals between the acts to express their opinion of
the players and of their respective parts. Sir Roger
hearing a cluster of them praise Orestes, struck in
with them, and told them that he thought his friend
Pylades was a very sensible man; as they were afterwards applauding Pyrrhus, Sir Roger put in a second time: "And let me tell you," says he, "though
he speaks but little, I like the old fellow in whiskers
as well as any of them." Captain Sentry seeing
two or three wags, who sat near us, lean with an
attentive ear towards Sir Roger, and fearing lest
they should smoke the Knight, plucked him by the
elbow, and whispered something in his ear, that lasted
till the opening of the fifth act. The Knight was
wonderfully attentive to the account which Orestes
gives of Pyrrhus his death, and at the conclusion of
it, told me it was such a bloody piece of work that
he was glad it was not done upon the stage. Seeing
afterwards Orestes in his raving fit, he grew more

than ordinary serious, and took occasion to moralize (in his way) upon an evil conscience, adding, that Orestes, in his madness, looked as if he saw something.

As we were the first that came into the house, so we were the last that went out of it; being resolved to have a clear passage for our old friend, whom we did not care to venture among the jostling of the crowd. Sir Roger went out fully satisfied with his entertainment, and we guarded him to his lodgings in the same manner that we brought him to the playhouse; being highly pleased, for my own part, not only with the performance of the excellent piece which had been presented, but with the satisfaction which it had given to the good old man.

XXXIII. WILL HONEYCOMB'S ADVENTURES.

Torva leæna lupum sequitur, lupus ipse capellam ;
Florentem cytisum sequitur lasciva capella.[1]

VIRGIL, *Eclogues,* ii. 63, 64.

As we were at the Club last night, I observed that my friend Sir Roger, contrary to his usual custom, sat very silent, and instead of minding what was said by the company, was whistling to himself in a very thoughtful mood, and playing with a cork. I jogged Sir Andrew Freeport, who sat between us; and as we were both observing him, we saw the Knight shake his head, and heard him say to himself, "A foolish woman! I can't believe it." Sir Andrew gave him a gentle pat upon the shoulder, and offered to lay him a bottle of wine that he was thinking of

1. The savage lioness hunts the wolf ; the wolf the kid pursues ;
   And now the frisky kid seeks for the flowering clover.

the Widow. My old friend started, and recovering
out of his brown study, told Sir Andrew that once in
his life he had been in the right. In short, after
some little hesitation, Sir Roger told us in the fulness of his heart, that he had just received a letter
from his steward, which acquainted him that his old
rival and antagonist in the county, Sir David Dun-
drum, had been making a visit to the Widow.
"However," says Sir Roger, "I can never think that
she 'll have a man that 's half a year older than I
am, and a noted Republican into the bargain."

Will Honeycomb, who looks upon love as his particular province, interrupting our friend with a jaunty
laugh; "I thought, Knight," says he, "thou hadst
lived long enough in the world not to pin thy happiness upon one that is a woman and a widow. I
think that without vanity I may pretend to know
as much of the female world as any man in Great
Britain, though the chief of my knowledge consists
in this, that they are not to be known." Will immediately, with his usual fluency, rambled into an
account of his own amours. "I am now," says he,
"upon the verge of fifty" (though, by the way, we
all knew he was turned of threescore). "You may
easily guess," continued Will, "that I have not lived
so long in the world without having had some
thoughts of settling in it, as the phrase is. To tell
you truly, I have several times tried my fortune that
way, though I can't much boast of my success.

"I made my first addresses to a young lady in the
country; but when I thought things were pretty well
drawing to a conclusion, her father happening to
hear that I had formerly boarded with a surgeon, the
old put forbid me his house, and within a fortnight

after married his daughter to a foxhunter in the neighborhood.

"I made my next applications to a widow, and attacked her so briskly, that I thought myself within a fortnight of her. As I waited upon her one morning, she told me that she intended to keep her ready money and jointure in her own hand, and desired me to call upon her attorney in Lyon's Inn, who would adjust with me what it was proper for me to add to it. I was so rebuffed by this overture, that I never inquired either for her or her attorney afterwards.

"A few months after I addressed myself to a young lady who was an only daughter, and of a good family: I danced with her at several balls, squeezed her by the hand, said soft things to her, and, in short, made no doubt of her heart; and, though my fortune was not equal to hers, I was in hopes that her fond father would not deny her the man she had fixed her affections upon. But as I went one day to the house in order to break the matter to him, I found the whole family in confusion, and heard, to my unspeakable surprise, that Miss Jenny was that very morning run away with the butler.

"I then courted a second widow, and am at a loss to this day how I came to miss her, for she had often commended my person and behavior. Her maid, indeed, told me one day that her mistress had said she never saw a gentleman with such a spindle pair of legs as Mr. Honeycomb.

"After this I laid siege to four heiresses successively, and being a handsome young dog in those days, quickly made a breach in their hearts; but I don't know how it came to pass, though I seldom failed of getting the daughters' consent, I could never in my life get the old people on my side.

"I could give you an account of a thousand other unsuccessful attempts, particularly of one which I made some years since upon an old woman, whom I had certainly borne away with flying colors, if her relations had not come pouring in to her assistance from all parts of England; nay, I believe I should have got her at last, had not she been carried off by an hard frost."

As Will's transitions are extremely quick, he turned from Sir Roger, and, applying himself to me, told me there was a passage in the book [1] I had considered last Saturday, which deserved to be writ in letters of gold; and taking out a pocket Milton, read the following lines, which are part of one of Adam's speeches to Eve after the fall: —

> Oh! why did God,
> Creator wise, that peopled highest heav'n
> With spirits masculine, create at last
> This novelty on earth, this fair defect
> Of Nature, and not fill the world at once
> With men, as angels, without feminine,
> Or find some other way to generate
> Mankind? This mischief had not then befall'n,
> And more that shall befall; innumerable
> Disturbances on earth through female snares,
> And straight conjunction with this sex : for either
> He never shall find out fit mate, but such
> As some misfortune brings him, or mistake :
> Or, whom he wishes most shall seldom gain,
> Through her perverseness; but shall see her gain'd
> By a far worse; or if she love, withheld
> By parents; or his happiest choice too late
> Shall meet, already link'd and wedlock bound
> To a fell adversary, his hate or shame;
> Which infinite calamity shall cause
> To human life, and household peace confound.[2]

1. Addison had been and still was publishing in *The Spectator* a series of detailed comment and criticism on Milton's *Paradise Lost*. He had just discussed Book x.

2. *Paradise Lost*, x. 888–908.

Sir Roger listened to this passage with great attention, and desiring Mr. Honeycomb to fold down a leaf at the place, and lend him his book, the Knight put it up in his pocket, and told us that he would read over those verses again before he went to bed.

XXXIV. SIR ROGER AT SPRING GARDEN.

Criminibus debent Hortos.[1]

JUVENAL, *Satires*, i. 75.

As I was sitting in my chamber and thinking on a subject for my next "Spectator," I heard two or three irregular bounces at my landlady's door, and upon the opening of it, a loud cheerful voice inquiring whether the philosopher was at home. The child who went to the door answered very innocently, that he did not lodge there. I immediately recollected that it was my good friend Sir Roger's voice; and that I had promised to go with him on the water[1] to Spring Garden, in case it proved a good evening. The Knight put me in mind of my promise from the bottom of the staircase, but told me that if I was speculating he would stay below till I had done. Upon my coming down, I found all the children of the family got about my old friend, and my landlady herself, who is a notable prating gossip, engaged in a conference with him, being mightily pleased with his stroking her little boy upon the head, and bidding him be a good child, and mind his book.

1. They owe their gardens to vice.
2. That is, by the Thames, which was a favorite way to more remote parts of the city. The Spring Gardens was the name of a pleasure resort on the Surrey or south side of the Thames, later more famous under its name of Vauxhall.

We were no sooner come to the Temple Stairs,[1] but we were surrounded with a crowd of watermen, offering us their respective services. Sir Roger, after having looked about him very attentively, spied one with a wooden leg, and immediately gave him orders to get his boat ready. As we were walking towards it, "You must know," says Sir Roger, "I never make use of anybody to row me, that has not either lost a leg or an arm. I would rather bate him a few strokes of his oar than not employ an honest man that has been wounded in the Queen's service. If I was a lord or a bishop, and kept a barge, I would not put a fellow in my livery that had not a wooden leg."

My old friend, after having seated himself, and trimmed the boat with his coachman, who, being a very sober man, always serves for ballast on these occasions, we made the best of our way for Vauxhall.[2] Sir Roger obliged the waterman to give us the history of his right leg, and hearing that he had left it at La Hogue,[3] with many particulars which passed in that glorious action, the Knight, in the triumph of his heart, made several reflections on the greatness of the British nation; as, that one Englishman could beat three Frenchmen; that we could never be in danger of Popery so long as we took care of our fleet; that the Thames was the noblest river in Europe; that London Bridge was a greater piece of work than any of the seven wonders of the world: with many other honest prejudices which naturally cleave to the heart of a true Englishman.

1. A landing on the Thames near the Temple.
2. That is the bridge of that name.
3. Twenty years before, May 19, 1692, the combined English and Dutch fleets had defeated the French at La Hogue, on the northwest coast of France.

After some short pause, the old Knight turning about his head twice or thrice, to take a survey of this great Metropolis, bid me observe how thick the city was set with churches, and that there was scarce a single steeple on this side Temple Bar. "A most heathenish sight!" says Sir Roger; "there is no religion at this end of the town. The fifty new churches will very much mend the prospect; but church work is slow, church work is slow!"

I do not remember I have anywhere mentioned, in Sir Roger's character, his custom of saluting everybody that passes by him with a good-morrow or a good-night. This the old man does out of the overflowings of his humanity, though at the same time it renders him so popular among all his country neighbors, that it is thought to have gone a good way in making him once or twice knight of the shire. He cannot forbear this exercise of benevolence even in town, when he meets with any one in his morning or evening walk. It broke from him to several boats that passed by us upon the water; but to the Knight's great surprise, as he gave the good-night to two or three young fellows a little before our landing, one of them, instead of returning the civility asked us, what queer old put we had in the boat, with a great deal of the like Thames ribaldry. Sir Roger seemed a little shocked at first, but at length, assuming a face of magistracy, told us that if he were a Middlesex justice, he would make such vagrants know that Her Majesty's subjects were no more to be abused by water than by land.

We were now arrived at Spring Garden, which is exquisitely pleasant at this time of year. When I considered the fragrancy of the walks and bowers,

with the choirs of birds that sang upon the trees, and
the loose tribe of people that walked under their
shades, I could not but look upon the place as a kind
of Mahometan paradise. Sir Roger told me it put
him in mind of a little coppice by his house in the
country, which his chaplain used to call an aviary
of nightingales. "You must understand," says the
Knight, "there is nothing in the world that pleases a
man in love so much as your nightingale. Ah, Mr.
Spectator! the many moonlight nights that I have
walked by myself, and thought on the Widow by the
music of the nightingales!" He here fetched a deep
sigh, and was falling into a fit of musing, when a
mask,[1] who came behind him, gave him a gentle tap
upon the shoulder, and asked him if he would drink
a bottle of mead with her. But the Knight being
startled at so unexpected a familiarity, and displeased
to be interrupted in his thoughts of the Widow, told
her she was a wanton baggage, and bid her go about
her business.

We concluded our walk with a glass of Burton ale
and a slice of hung beef. When we had done eating
ourselves, the Knight called a waiter to him, and bid
him carry the remainder to the waterman that had
but one leg. I perceived the fellow stared upon him
at the oddness of the message, and was going to be
saucy; upon which I ratified the Knight's commands
with a peremptory look.

1. A woman wearing a mask, a common appurtenance at the
time. It has been refined down to a veil in these days.

XXXV. DEATH OF SIR ROGER DE COVERLEY.[1]

Heu Pietas! heu prisca Fides! [2]

VIRGIL, *Æneid*, vi. 878.

WE last night received a Piece of ill News at our Club, which very sensibly afflicted every one of us. I question not but my Readers themselves will be troubled at the hearing of it. To keep them no longer in Suspence, Sir ROGER DE COVERLEY *is dead.*[3] He departed this Life at his House in the Country, after a few Weeks Sickness. Sir ANDREW FREEPORT has a Letter from one of his Correspondents in those Parts, that informs him the old Man caught a Cold at the County-Sessions, as he was very warmly promoting an Address of his own penning, in which he succeeded according to his Wishes. But this Particular comes from a Whig-Justice of Peace, who was always Sir ROGER'S Enemy and Antagonist. I have Letters both from the Chaplain and Captain *Sentry* which mention nothing of it, but are filled with many Particulars to the Honour of the good old Man. I have likewise a Letter from the Butler, who took so much care of me last Summer when I was at the Knight's House. As my Friend the Butler mentions, in the Simplicity of his Heart, several Circumstances the others have passed over in Silence, I shall give my Reader a Copy of his Letter, without any Alteration or Diminution.

1. As explained in the introduction, this number of *The Spectator* is reproduced with the spelling, italics, and capitalization originally used.

2. Ah piety! ah ancient faith!

3. The anticipated closing of *The Spectator* doubtless determined Addison to put the good knight to death. Writers of the time assert that Addison feared the character might otherwise be adopted by some other writer.

Honoured Sir,

'Knowing that you was[1] my old Master's good
'Friend, I could not forbear sending you the melan-
'choly News of his Death, which has afflicted the
'whole Country, as well as his poor Servants, who
'loved him, I may say, better than we did our Lives.
'I am afraid he caught his Death the last County
'Sessions, where he would go to see Justice done to a
'poor Widow Woman, and her Fatherless Children,
'that had been wronged by a neighbouring Gentle-
'man; for you know, Sir, my good Master was al-
'ways the poor Man's Friend. Upon his coming
'home, the first Complaint he made was, that he had
'lost his Roast-Beef Stomach, not being able to touch
'a Sirloin, which was served up according to Custom;
'and you know he used to take great Delight in it.
'From that time forward he grew worse and worse,
'but still kept a good Heart to the last. Indeed we
'were once in great Hope of his Recovery, upon a
'kind Message that was sent him from the Widow
'Lady whom he had made love to the Forty last
'Years of his Life; but this only proved a Light'ning
'before Death. He has bequeathed to this Lady, as
'a token of his Love, a great Pearl Necklace, and a
'Couple of Silver Bracelets set with Jewels, which
'belonged to my good old Lady his Mother: He has
'bequeathed the fine white Gelding, that he used to
'ride a hunting upon, to his Chaplain, because he
'thought he would be kind to him, and has left you
'all his Books. He has, moreover, bequeathed to
'the Chaplain a very pretty Tenement with good

1. Not necessarily to be referred to the butler's ignorance of
good English, for the locution was common enough amongst well-
educated men at this time.

'Lands about it. It being a very cold Day when he
'made his Will, he left for Mourning, to every Man
'in the Parish, a great Frize-Coat, and to every
'Woman a black Riding-hood. It was a most mov-
'ing Sight to see him take leave of his poor Servants,
'commending us all for our Fidelity, whilst we were
'not able to speak a Word for weeping. As we
'most of us are grown Gray-headed in our Dear
'Master's Service, he has left us Pensions and Lega-
'cies, which we may live very comfortably upon, the
'remaining part of our Days. He has bequeath'd a
'great deal more in Charity, which is not yet come to
'my Knowledge, and it is peremptorily said in the
'Parish, that he has left Mony to build a Steeple to
'the Church; for he was heard to say some time ago,
'that if he lived two Years longer, *Coverly* Church
'should have a Steeple to it. The Chaplain tells
'every body that he made a very good End, and
'never speaks of him without Tears. He was bur-
'ied, according to his own Directions, among the
'Family of the *Coverly's*, on the Left Hand of his
'father Sir *Arthur*. The Coffin was carried by Six
'of his Tenants, and the Pall held up by Six of the
' *Quorum:* The whole Parish follow'd the Corps with
'heavy Hearts, and in their Mourning Suits, the
'Men in Frize, and the Women in Riding-Hoods.
'Captain SENTRY, my Master's Nephew, has taken
'Possession of the Hall-House, and the whole Estate.[1]

1. Steele in *The Spectator* for November 24, 1712, makes a
sort of postscript to this whole affair of Sir Roger by producing a letter from Captain Sentry, written from Coverley Hall,
Worcestershire, in which he says : " I am come to the succession
of the estate of my honored kinsman, Sir Roger de Coverley ;
and I assure you I find it no easy task to keep up the figure of

'When my old Master saw him a little before his
'Death, he shook him by the Hand, and wished him
'Joy of the Estate which was falling to him, desiring
'him only to make good Use of it, and to pay the
'several Legacies, and the Gifts of Charity which he
'told him he had left as Quitrents upon the Estate.
'The Captain truly seems a courteous Man, though
'he says but little. He makes much of those whom
'my Master loved, and shows great Kindness to the
'old House-dog, that you know my poor Master was
'so fond of. It would have gone to your Heart to
'have heard the Moans the dumb Creature made on
'the Day of my Master's Death. He has ne'er joyed
'himself since; no more has any of us. 'T was the
'melancholiest Day for the poor People that ever
'happened in *Worcestershire*. This being all from,

   Honoured Sir,
  Your most Sorrowful Servant,
       Edward Biscuit.

'*P. S.* My Master desired, some Weeks before
'he died, that a Book which comes up to you by the

master of the fortune which was so handsomely enjoyed by that
honest plain man. I cannot (with respect to the great obliga-
tions I have, be it spoken) reflect upon his character, but I am
confirmed in the truth which I have, I think, heard spoken at
the club, to wit, that a man of a warm and well-disposed heart
with a very small capacity, is highly superior in human society
to him who with the greatest talents, is cold and languid in his
affections. But alas ! why do I make a difficulty in speaking of
my worthy ancestor's failings ? His little absurdities and incapacity for the conversation of the politest men are dead with
him, and his greater qualities are even now useful to him. I
know not whether by naming those disabilities I do not enhance
his merit, since he has left behind him a reputation in his country which would be worth the pains of the wisest man's whole
life to arrive at."

'Carrier should be given to Sir *Andrew Freeport,*
'in his Name.'

    This Letter, notwithstanding the poor Butler's
Manner of writing it, gave us such an Idea of our
good old Friend, that upon the reading of it there
was not a dry Eye in the Club. Sir *Andrew* opening the Book, found it to be a Collection of Acts of
Parliament. There was in particular the Act of
Uniformity, with some Passages in it marked by Sir
Roger's own Hand. Sir *Andrew* found that they
related to two or three Points, which he had disputed
with Sir *Roger* the last time he appeared at the
Club. Sir *Andrew*, who would have been merry at
such an Incident on another Occasion, at the sight of
the old Man's Hand-writing burst into Tears, and
put the Book into his Pocket. Captain *Sentry* informs me, that the Knight has left Rings and Mourning for every one in the Club.

INDEX.

www.ingramcontent.com/pod-product-compliance
Lightning Source LLC
Chambersburg PA
CBHW031428250626
47155CB00004B/1663